MOTOCROSS
& OFF-ROAD TRAINING HANDBOOK

Tune Your Body for Race-Winning Performance

MOTOCROSS
& OFF-ROAD TRAINING HANDBOOK

Tune Your Body for Race-Winning Performance

MARK THOMPSON

MOTORBOOKS

ACKNOWLEDGMENTS

There may be only one name on the front cover, but no author ever writes a book without a lot of help. Here's my list:

This book is dedicated to my mother, for a lifetime of inspiration, love, and support. You're the one who turned me into a reader and writer.

My wife Carole and daughter Stephanie for their love and help.

My many racing buddies and fellow competitors, but especially Harry Gooch, Jim Denevan, Woody Graves and his daughter Savannah, Ted Simmons, and Paul Boyer—you're the people who make going racing as much fun as it is, so the beer is on me next time!

Maryann Turner, my trusted assistant and persistent researcher.

Tom "Son of a Nun" Goddard for being such a great photo model.

Andy "A.A." McIntyre for his photo assistance.

Dr. Scott Slivka for reviewing the injury chapter (my shoulder's fine, now, doc).

Billy Barrett for the first edit and general advice.

World Gym and Beckett Ridge Country Club, both in West Chester, Ohio, for the use of their facilities and equipment during photo shoots.

And last, but certainly not least, to Lee Klancher, my editor at MBI. Lee shepherded this project along from planning to final printing.

Thanks to all of you. This book wouldn't exist without your help, support, occasional nagging, and encouragement.

First published in 2006 by Motorbooks, an imprint of MBI Publishing Company, Galtier Plaza, Suite 200, 380 Jackson Street, St. Paul, MN 55101-3885 USA

Copyright © 2006 by Mark Thompson

MBI Publishing Company titles are also available at discounts in bulk quantity for industrial or sales-promotional use. For details write to Special Sales Manager at MBI Publishing Company, Galtier Plaza, Suite 200, 380 Jackson Street, St. Paul, MN 55101-3885 USA

ISBN-13: 978-0-7603-2113- 3
ISBN-10: 0-7603-2113- 2

On the frontispiece: Nate Ramsey at work in the gym. *Joe Bonnello*

On the title page: On the line at Spring Creek MX track. *Mark Thompson*

On the back cover: Specific excercises are important to a winning motocross training regime. *Mark Thompson*

Editor: Lee Klancher
Designer: Kou Lor

Printed in China

About the author

Mark Thompson long ago figured out he was put on earth to do two things: race motorcycles and write about racing. He's been at it ever since, having raced thousands of laps in a dozen states, along with riding many enduros, hare scrambles, ice racing, and a bit of asphalt fun roadracing. An active racer, he puts down laps in both modern motocross and in AHRMA vintage motocross. He's been a contributor to dozens of publications, editor of two motorcycle magazines, and publisher of another, as well as Managing Editor for *Readers' Digest* Special Interest Publications. A lifetime jock, gym rat, and coach, he's completed 10 marathons and hundreds of other running races. Originally from Wisconsin, he now lives in West Chester, Ohio. To contact him or for more training advice and answers to your questions, visit www.motocrosscoach.com

CONTENTS

INTRODUCTION

We're racers. That makes us different from the typical guy. We're a whole lot more athletic because we're participating in a risky sport. We know we must train to be in good shape for racing, but the hows and whys of the training makes for a complex and confusing topic.

Over the years, there have been a number of motocross conditioning manuals published, usually written by well-known pro riders or their training gurus. I've probably read them all. You may have too. Unfortunately, they all have one major flaw: They're written as if everyone is a pro rider who can dedicate most of his day to training. For professional athletes, it's a full-time job and that's the only way they know how to approach training.

While the advice might be great if you fit into that niche, it's simply not the real world. The real world is about 200 card-carrying AMA Pro motocross riders—most of whom you've never heard of and never will—and a million-plus amateur motocross and off-road riders. The elite riders are the exception. You, me, and your riding buddies are the real-world norm. I'm a big fan of reality. You should be too, and that's why this book is different. The training advice in these pages is based on what real people can accomplish within a normal schedule. As much fun as it

would be (for a while, anyway) to live in that fantasy world where we can train all day, it's just not going to happen.

The real world means having your day filled with the demands of work, school, commuting, business trips, lousy weather (not everybody lives in SoCal), kids and spouses, friends and their problems, lawns and houses, and all the million other things that eat up a day. Finding an hour to train each day is just another chore on a long list of gotta-do stuff.

This book will give you a road map through all the complexities and outright misinformation about training, nutrition, finding the time to train, getting enough rest, workout planning, injuries, and race weekends. This book is a real-world guide to getting into the best shape of your racing life within the limits of an average guy's schedule. Most of the work outs in this book can be done within 60 to 90 minutes, an amount of time we can reasonably slot into our schedules on a regular basis.

If you want to win, you have to train. *Kawasaki*

The training in this book is for you, the average Joe racer.

Joe Average Racer

Joe Average racer is the forgotten man in off-road racing's growth. Motocross is the world's most popular amateur motor sport—but I believe that all the emphasis should be placed on the word *amateur*. It's the only motor sport that the Average Joe can get into and enjoy on an average income. You can throw a leg over a competitive race bike for $5,000 ($4,000 if you buy it one-year-used), and your bank's friendly loan officer will be thrilled to allow you to have all this fun for only 48 monthly easy-for-your-wife-to-digest payments. Motocross is cheaper than buying most boats, and a lot more fun.

Of course, it helps if you have a lot of extra income to burn, but even if you had a key to Microsoft's vaults, you're not going to crack the pro ranks without that rare combination of talent, ability, training, hard work, and exceptional fitness. What makes motocross a true everyman's sport is that it's the only motor sport where having cubic bucks doesn't mean anything beyond having nicer toys. Unlike auto racing, where

the more money you spend the more speed you get in return, you can't buy a championship in motocross. You have to physically work for it.

You know you need to train, but the question is always what training to do. Pro riders and wannabe-pros hire personal trainers to help them stay focused on a rigorous training program that delivers the results, but few of us have that option.

Think of this book as your personal trainer.

But I Already Train

Already doing a fair amount of training? Good for you! Keep it up.

But, I'll let you in on a secret: you're probably wasting a big chunk of your training time. Unless you're following a sports-specific training plan, your work outs are probably the ones that you find fun or easy to do rather than the ones that will help make you faster on a motocross bike. Most of us waste our training time because we don't follow a detailed training plan.

Case in point: My good racing buddy got into skinny-tire road bicycles in a big way and he figured it had to help his racing. To some extent, he was right. He worked hard at bicycling, went on group long-distance rides, bought an exotic carbon fiber road bike with all the goodies (peddle-bikers have Gearhead Flu as bad as motocrossers), and kept his legs cranking away on those pedals for a couple million repetitions through good weather and bad. After a year of this hard work, his pulse rate was low, he'd lost weight, looked good, his aerobic capacity was way up . . . and his legs were still getting tired at the three-lap point in the first moto!

Why? Because his training was excellent for riding a bicycle on asphalt, but it was only partially beneficial for turning laps through sandy whoops or hanging on over Volkswagen-sized braking bumps.

For athletic training to have value beyond general fitness, it has to be *sports specific*. Running, bicycling, or lifting weights will help your general fitness,

but past a certain level all it does is make you a better runner or bicyclist, not a better motocross racer.

What you need is a guide to motocross-specific training advice that teaches you how to design a personal training program that works within the time limits of your average, busy week. This book is your guide. I'm not going to assume you're going to spend six hours daily training or that you even know how to train. It doesn't matter what your level of fitness is today—I'll help you get the most out of your work outs.

Exercise Cults

The real question sometimes isn't what exercises you should do, but who you should believe.

Sports training is a relatively young field. You can find training guides dating back more than 100 years (the period between 1890 and 1910 was very big for endurance sports), but most of the research and facts about sports conditioning come from only the past 30 years or so. A lot of what we think we know is really just at the "good guess" stage of things, because the science behind it is still so new. Many of the most important questions about training are still unanswered. This is typical of science in all fields; it takes decades to accumulate the data, then additional decades to test various theories and measure the actual results.

This is why sports training is filled with so many conflicting programs, bad advice, and downright hucksters. There are very few concrete take-it-to-the-bank answers about a lot of training questions. Nobody is absolutely positive what the correct answers are to questions about diet and nutrition, whether you should do strength training at a normal speed or ultra-slow, if whether running strengthens knees or destroys them, and dozens more. If you spend any time studying the work out advice of even the most renowned trainers, it's easy to come away more confused than when you began.

The average guy just wants a program that works, period. He might be

MOTOCROSS AND OFF-ROAD . . .

While we refer mostly to motocross throughout this book, the training advice applies to all types of off-road riding, from enduros to just messing around in the dirt with anything wearing knobbies. For the purposes of this book, "motocross" is short-hand for any type of off-road riding.

impressed that Joe Somebody added 100 pounds of rock-hard muscle with just 17 minutes of training per week but most of us know that if it sounds too good to be true, it probably isn't. There's no independent agency out there saying this training method works and this one is garbage. Sports training has a lot in common with religion or politics, especially if you want to get an argument going. Battles get fought over the opposing work out philosophies.

As I said, the real question for you isn't what to do, but who to believe.

Here are my credentials: lifetime jock and gym rat, lifetime and still active motocross and cross-country racer from back when Maico and CZ made the hot moto-weapons to the latest crop of four-stroke moto-weapons. Certified professional trainer and coach (less of a big deal than you'd think), multi-time marathon finisher, and thoroughly determined researcher. I'm a full-time cynic when it comes to training advice, testing new ideas personally. If I've learned anything from decades of training, it's that there are some basic concepts that get ignored in the search for something more glamorous.

I believe that training, in order to be effective and real-world, has to be personalized as much as possible. You're a smart person—you bought this book, didn't you? You can make smart decisions about the training you need, and most importantly, select the training methods you'll stick with so you can reap the most benefits.

Who Needs This Book?

A lot of training guidelines assume you're already in good shape. That's wrong. If you have the strength to pick up this book and flip the pages, I can help you design a training program that fits your current level of fitness and your schedule.

If you're one of those lucky people who can easily ride your race bike every day for a couple of hours, then do that instead. There's no better training for racing a dirt bike than riding a lot. You'll develop the necessary muscles, reflexes, and endurance quicker with a handlebar in front of you and the throttle twisted open, than you will doing sit-ups in a gym.

However, even if you have a motocross track in your backyard and a fleet of bikes to choose from, I'd still recommend studying the sections on diet, injuries, arm pump, and improving your reflexes. Or ignore everything else, but still make it a point to read the chapter on Eating to Win. Sad to say, but the standard American diet is the single biggest obstacle to maintaining good health and building strength.

How this Book Works

Look for this image sprinkled throughout the book:

There's not much time when the two-minute board goes up, so you'd better be paying attention. Same deal here. These are fast bits of information from that chapter in bite-size, easy-to-remember form. You still need to read the whole chapter, but the Two-Minute Board summary makes for a convenient reference. Think of them as nonfattening informational snacks.

Political Non-Correctness

I refused to fight the political correctness war a long time ago. I love women and especially women riders—my daughter is one—but face it, around 99

Everybody can race, but not everybody is male. But as far as the language in this book is concerned, we're not going to worry about gender.

percent of the motocross racers, off-road riders, and dirt bike play riders are male. Rather than wear out my fingers typing "he/she" or searching for gender-neutral terms, I wrote this book in pure American male idiom. The training advice is the same no matter what the color of your leathers.

TWO-MINUTE BOARD

- This is a training manual for the rest of us.
- Real-world advice you can use.
- You're probably wasting a good portion of your training time.
- Exercise cults and how to decide who to trust. One clue: Start with a real racer.
- How to tell if you need this book or not.

Chapter 1

WHY TRAIN?

Why train? It seems like a simple question.

But really, why should a dirt bike racer have to train? After all, the bike does most of the hard work with the energy of those 30 to 50 horsepower tucked away inside the motor. You just twist the throttle and shift the gears—hardly tasks that require much strength or endurance.

Marathon runners and bicycle racers have no choice but to train hard, because they rely only on the power in their own legs and lungs. But dirt bikers? If you've got enough leg to kick the bike to life and enough muscle to hold onto the handlebars, you can enter a motocross or enduro. It doesn't matter to the other riders if you're dragging along a spare-tire waist and arms with flab wattles like an old lady's.

Why train? In order to be faster, stronger, healthier, more self-confident, and to reduce the chances of injury from our sometimes dangerous sport.

Staying in shape lets you race longer and live longer. What better reasons do you need?

Of course, we know we need to be in shape because controlling that caged-up horsepower when it's time to unleash it isn't as easy as people think. Guiding a moto-missile requires strength, endurance, balance, a good grip, and razor-sharp reflexes. You get, retain, and build those physical skills with a physical training program.

Now, you're not going to find many athletes of any caliber, whether they're world champs or weekend jocks, who will claim that training is fun, a sheer delight, and something they'd do no matter what the cost, hassle, or effort. The boring reality is that staying in shape is work, plain and simple.

This isn't to say people don't want to be athletically fit and trim. There are few better feelings in life than piloting a muscular, healthy body. Everybody *wants* to be in shape, with clean arteries, strong lungs, muscular legs, sharper thinking, enhanced disease resistance, and all the other benefits of being in good physical shape. Still, hardly anyone is enthusiastic about actually doing the training that will give them those benefits. Humans just aren't like that.

Lazy is as Lazy Does

The problem is that humans by their basic nature are as lazy as overfed poodles. The human body *wants* to take it easy; it doesn't like hard work. Programmed into our genetic heritage are instructions to only work hard until the necessities of life are present and then shift into neutral and coast. Once there's enough fat stored away to get us through the next few days, our inner programming tells us to take it easy and conserve energy, not burn it. We'd rather sit than walk; walk than run; coast than pedal; float than backstroke. Working out isn't logical in terms that the body readily understands, appreciates, or gets gung-ho about.

Don't take being called lazy as an insult. It's just a fact you need to work with, just like knowing the air pressure in your bike's tires or what octane fuel to buy. It's normal for people to look for the easiest way to accomplish something, because that's what evolution has taught us to do. It's the reason we developed big brains to compensate for our puny muscles. For most of humankind's existence, hard work was necessary to simply sustain life—or avoid becoming lunch for a saber-toothed tiger by outrunning it. The concept of intentionally working to build muscles and endurance is a relatively recent concept, dating back to the late 1800s when the industrial revolution was in full stride and sedentary occupations had started to become the norm. In the big picture, we're all new at this—learning how to do something that doesn't come naturally.

Even though I've been a jock all of my happily misspent life, I'm also the first to tell people that if medical science came up with a miracle vaccine that would keep me in a permanent state of fitness, I'd elbow my way to the front of the line to get the shot. No more having to sacrifice two hours daily to sweating and straining, pushing weary legs another mile, or carefully weighing what having another beer is going to cost me in sweat equity the next day. Any jock will tell you about days when a biting wind, swirling snow, or rain drops the size of golf balls makes being outside an act of lunacy. But we do it anyhow.

Being fit is a choice and only one person can make that choice for you. It's completely up to you whether you're in shape or not. Reading this or any book

Getting stronger lets you ride faster, longer, and under more control. You can be—and should be!—as fast on the last lap as you were on the first lap.

won't do it. All I can provide is direction and some nudges in the right direction. You have to provide the work ethic, motivation and stubbornness to succeed. You have to choose to trade a chunk of your spare time for the opportunity to sweat, get blisters, pulverize your muscles, vomit from heat exhaustion, shiver in sub-zero winters, and tattoo your skin with bits of gravel from bicycle crashes. That's reality.

Training for Life

While this book is about getting you into the best shape of your life so you can be faster and more confident on a motocross track, the training philosophy I hope you learn from me is more basic: You train for life, not just for motocross.

Most sports training advice has you following a rollercoaster program where you start at the bottom, work your way up to a peak, and then roar back to the bottom, losing a lot of hard-earned fitness in the process. Then next season you do it all over again. Sorry, but that's nuts and not a very good use of your time. What I preach is that you get fit and then you stay that way, skipping the whole rollercoaster routine.

The exercises in these pages will make you a stronger, fitter, better-prepared racer, but fitness should be a goal in itself, not tied to any specific sport. What if you get bored with the sport, or injured, or your wife makes you choose between racing and being married? What I hope you'll take away from this book is an approach to living an athletic and healthy lifestyle that you can maintain your whole life, whether you keep on

There are plenty of diet, fitness, training, muscle-building, lifestyle, and workout books out there. The question is whose advice do you believe?

racing or not. Lots of people train for specific sports, only to drop out and stop training. Don't let that happen to you.

The Benefits Package

Reasons to train? There are lots of them:

• You're less likely to get injured and the injury will probably be less severe.

• If you do get hurt, being in shape means you recover quicker.

• You can finally explore the real capabilities of your motorcycle and see what it's really like to unleash 50 horse-power down the front straight or through the whoops.

• Gaining strength and endurance will let you ride longer and faster under more control.

• Riding longer and faster translates into doing better—if you can out-last someone, you don't need to be any faster than he is—just pass him when he gets tired.

• More strength and less flab means you feel better about yourself; boosting your self-confidence, an essential ingredient in any successful racer.

• You'll have more and better sex.

• Fewer colds and other nuisance diseases and a quicker recovery when you do catch a bug.

• You'll sleep better and wake up feeling more rested.

• Your overall health will improve, often to the point where you can stop taking any medications.

• You'll be able to take all those "Where Do You Place?" tests of physical ability and score so far above normal

DO THIS FIRST!

Before starting any physical training program, get a complete physical exam by your doctor. You're going to be pushing your body hard and your doctor can tell you whether it's up to it or not. You need a physical exam whether you're a teenager or a full-fledged, licensed adult. Since you're probably male, you're probably also good at skipping doctor's appointments. Don't do that! Go, get it over with, and get the news—good or bad. One reason women live longer than men in our society is that they go to the doctor more often for check-ups.

Getting and staying in shape should be a lifetime goal. There's no off-season in life. Start young, get strong, stay that way. *Kawasaki Motors*

you'll look like you're cheating—being in "normal" shape is a pretty low-level goal.

• You'll be able to focus better on work, school, and life in general.

• As you get in better shape, it becomes easier to do what's necessary to lead a healthy life.

• You'll be an inspiration to others; your kids, your parents, your spouse, your racing buddies, your employers.

Health benefits that are almost too numerous to list: less heart disease, stronger joints, less risk of osteoporosis, less body fat, less bad cholesterol, lower blood pressure, a better attitude (exercise helps prevent depression), reduced chance of developing diabetes, fewer everyday injuries, less back pain.

Yeah, but What about That Butt-Blaster Gadget on TV?

Watch TV for more than 10 minutes and you'll see a few dozen ads for miracle weight-loss devices, miracle diet foods, miracle muscle developers, miracle diet plans, and of course the always-popular six-pack-abs in only 20 minutes a day.

It's a miraculous world out there in TV-land.

For sure, we'd all have a lot more spare time if even one of these products actually worked as promised. No more need to run 25 miles this week . . . just pop a pill. Want seconds on dessert tonight? No problem, because

DOING THE MATH

A lifetime spent working out, using just an hour every day as a minimum (and it's a very average minimum), adds up to just 15 days a year, and not even a half-year's time (152 days) in a decade. Maybe that sounds like a lot, but it's really not. C'mon, you already spend ten times more than that just watching TV.

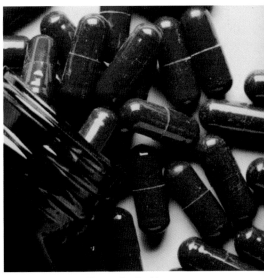

If you're taking pills to deal with various medical conditions, getting into shape may be the medicine you *really* need. By following a solid work out program, it's likely you can get off the prescription drug merry-go-round.

Racers win because of a lot of factors. In motocross, your level of conditioning and strength is a major element in the trophy-grabbing sweepstakes. But, you still have to learn how to ride fast. *iStockphoto.com*

tomorrow you can just follow the latest grapefruit and sauerkraut diet plan. Muscles like Arnold? An easy 20 minutes of sweat-free exercise on this gadget, that fits under your bed and doubles as a carpet shampooer. I love how nobody ever sweats in these ads, the exercise device is set up in a luxurious home instead of a musty basement, and everything gets demonstrated by hunky dudes and bodacious babes.

While some of the exercise machines do offer actual training benefits, it's never as quick and easy as the ads claim. For the amount you have to pay to own just one of these devices, you can have a health club membership for a couple of years with access to the many exercise machines, free weights, and other benefits the club offers.

The standard advice applies to anything that sounds too good to be true, especially when it comes to miracle training or diet results. If it sounds too good to be true, buy with caution.

A Ticket on the Reality Bus

Allow me to give you a ride on the Reality Bus. Training for a high-intensity sport such as motocross or for that matter, any other real sport, is plain, old-fashioned hard work.

There aren't any shortcuts.

There aren't any miracle training

devices, safe designer drugs, or goofy diets that will transform you from a lard-filled couch potato to a muscled stud with only a few minutes of gentle effort.

It's going to take more than 20 minutes a day. A lot more.

There are going to be days when you're ready to quit your training, sell the race bike, and take up miniature golf.

Working out is not easy and it's often not going to be much fun, especially at the beginning.

To be effective, you never stop training your whole life.

There is no off-season.

Training can be as boring and tedious as the worst job you ever had, or could imagine having.

Because training is hard, it's really easy to quit and nobody will know you're a quitter—except you.

You're going to sweat (a lot), struggle (a bit), hit plateaus (that's the natural order of things), and have days when you'll scrape up every feeble excuse you can dream of to avoid your work out. That's reality.

As I promised at the beginning of this book, I'm big on reality and not

13

sugarcoating facts. There are plenty of exercise books out there that try convince you exercise can be easy, require minimal time and effort, and be more fun than tickling kittens. It would be nice if it were true, but it's not. To achieve the kind of results you can put to good use on a motocross track is going to require work.

The fun comes later. It comes from actually being in shape, not the getting there. It's a whole lot of fun when you can put those new muscles and lungs through their paces by pulling a monster holeshot and charging away from the pack. That's why you do all the work: to have more fun racing.

Most of us race because it's enjoyable and because we're the kind of people who like the challenge and thrill of doing something other people can't even imagine attempting. Fun as it may be, we can't ever forget that motocross is a difficult, physically challenging and demanding sport with very real dangers. People die racing or get horribly injured, some of them in life-altering ways. Being in shape lets you deal with both racing's intense physical demands and the effects of a nasty crash. Muscle is better protection in a crash than fat, and muscle also helps keep you from crashing in the first place. Think of your daily work out as buying racing health insurance, because that's what it adds up to.

Will This Book Make Me a Race Winner?

Does all of this hard training mean you'll automatically become a winning racer, fully sponsored and taking home trophies every weekend? Of course not. Get real, no one can promise you that.

To acquire those kinds of race-winning riding skills, you need to ride a lot, master the proper techniques, and work on your riding skills as hard as you've worked on your physical training. The muscle and endurance you add by following this book's advice makes doing that easier. With strength comes the ability to pick up the front of the bike and carry it through the whoops, and the endurance to continue doing it lap after lap.

Physical training is just part of a big race-winning package composed of unequal and totally random amounts of natural talent (you have it or you don't), large doses of luck, intense desire, fierce determination, and the fickle finger of fate—Roger DeCoster just happens to be walking by as you clear the triple and he signs you to the factory team. Without building a solid base of training and conditioning, the other things aren't very likely to happen.

Who Is This Book For?

This is a book about training for motocross or any other activity involving a dirt bike or ATV. Since I'm a motocross racer, I always think "motocross" and for the purposes of this book, that's shorthand for any kind of dirt bike racing. While I've raced enduros, flat track, cross-country, road races, and in the winter, ice racing, mentally I classify all of it as simply additional training for motocross. Adjust your personal reality accordingly.

This is not a riding techniques book. You won't learn how to seat-jump doubles or rail the berms. You *will* find out how to build the strength necessary so that you can learn and practice those techniques.

Is this training advice only for the super-serious hard-core racers?

Absolutely not. With a little help from me, you're going to actually design your own work outs to fit your goals, your needs, and your physical abilities. Nobody else can do that for you because no one else can do the training for you. If you're someone who play-rides in the dirt and just wants to be in decent shape for having fun, then this book will help you get there. If you're a moto-fanatic who dreams of bike-swallowing whoops sections and crowded first turns, I can help you develop a personal training program that will max out your endurance and strength levels. It's going to be your personal training plan because only one person can set the goals and do the

work necessary to meet them—that's you. You have to take responsibility. All I can do is coach.

By the way, the single best physical training for racing is to simply ride as much as possible. If you're already doing that, don't stop. But by a lot, I mean at least five hours per week, every week, in a situation where you can practice different techniques and technical skills. You're not allowed to include actual race days in this total and this can't be just riding around in circles, never really doing anything except burning gasoline. Riding as much as possible is the single best training for racing motocross, just as swimming a lot, pedaling a bicycle for hours, or skiing every day are the best ways to develop the muscles, balance, timing, and skills those sports require.

If you can ride a lot, do it! There's no better training. Then use this book to improve your diet and fine-tune your muscles and reflexes.

How Long Will It Take?

My personal training mantra has always been: "There Is No Off-Season." Your training never ends. Sorry about that.

Once you start to improve your strength and endurance, there's not really a point where you're officially done. Being in shape needs to be a lifetime commitment. It's not a goal with an end, but the whole point of your life and existence. You stop training and trying to lead a healthy life when you stop breathing.

That said, from a less philosophical perspective, to see a noticeable increase in your strength and endurance will require at least a couple of weeks of following your training plan, depending on where you're starting from in a physical sense. You didn't gain 20 pounds overnight and you're not going to lose it overnight either. Building muscle and endurance is the same deal. Everything happens slowly, which is why you have to keep at it.

Generally, you'll start to see the first few changes in your body in as little as about two weeks' time. They won't be big changes, but it will be just enough so that you'll feel like maybe there's a point to all this work. The changes will be subtle, not earthshaking, and they come in fits and starts.

Fitness improvements aren't linear, but more like a staircase. There's a noticeable bit of improvement, then a plateau that seems to last forever, followed by another big step up the stairs, and then another plateau. You'll notice most of the changes in the early months of your training, then as your fitness level ratchets up, it becomes harder to tell when you've gone up another notch.

Greatly summarized, here's what to expect in the first six months:

Month One: In the first few weeks of faithfully following your training program, you'll see and feel visible yet noticeable small improvements in your strength and endurance. The warm-up doesn't leave you worn out, and running or walking distances that once seemed impossible are now no big deal. Your clothes will start to fit better because you've erased a little of your flab and you may already have people complimenting you on your new look.

Month Two: I'm glad you were feeling good about your first month of effort, because the second month can be a major let-down. If you weigh yourself regularly, you may have regained some lost pounds. Don't worry about it. If

you've been faithfully following your training regimen, the regained weight is going to be added muscle, which is more dense than fat. Your waistline will maybe still shrink a bit more, but you may not see much change overall compared to the heady improvements of the first month. The second month is when most people give up on their diets, stop working out, and otherwise run up the white flag. But you need to stick it out because . . .

Month Three: If you've stuck to your training plan for eight weeks, the third month can be sweet. Your body has been adjusting to the added stresses of training, reworking muscles behind the scenes, reallocating body resources, and doing all kinds of internal repairs and renovations. Typically, the third month is when a lot of these changes kick in and become noticeable. You'll be proud of yourself, rightly so, and probably be hearing some compliments about your newfound speed and the way you finished the last lap without any signs of fading. Eat up the praise because . . .

Months Four through Six: These months are likely to be another plateau period. Your body has adjusted to the increased demands and now has a reservoir of endurance. Improvements in terms of miles run, weight lifted, or other measurements are showing few increases. That's the downside. The upside is that you're now in pretty solid shape, and if nothing else, your work outs are adding to and maintaining your fitness foundation.

Making a Big Deal about Diet

Over the years I've become convinced that the biggest obstacle to getting results from training and improving overall health comes down to what you're putting into your body. The typical American diet is a total disaster. It's killing people shortening lives, making them sick or dependent on prescription drugs, limiting their enjoyment of life, and limiting their success in sports. Two-thirds of the U.S. population is now obese—and a quarter of that number tip

Because the typical American diet is a nutritional and medical disaster, I'm going to make a big deal about proper diet in Chapter 5. Don't skip it! What you eat has a major effect on your training results, not to mention your overall health. Junk food = junk health.

the scales as grossly overweight. Our kids are as fat as their parents, with adolescent diabetes setting new records, and the U.S. military is having a hard time finding recruits that meet normal weight guidelines and are healthy enough to endure boot camp.

This is a national disgrace and a health crisis as severe as those associated with smoking. We should be ashamed of ourselves. I realized that I couldn't help you train without devoting time and space to diet. Just telling you to "eat right" doesn't tell you anything you don't already know, and it's a message that is easily ignored.

Don't just skim over Chapter 5: Eating to Win. It contains weight loss tips that actually do work and it clears up the confusion about what you should be eating. I want you to eat right because I want you to succeed. I want to make sure your physical gains from all the ass-busting hard work I'm going to throw at you, are reinforced by good, sound nutrition. Yeah, you *know* you need to eat right, but do you really understand what that means and what choices to make? You probably don't, so I'm going to tell you.

Training Advice: Who Do You Believe?

Giving training and diet advice is like talking about religion or politics: You're absolutely guaranteed of pissing off a lot of people.

Training has a lot of cults. There's plenty of loud and angry debate over who's really following the One True Faith. The great debate is the reason there are so many exercise and diet books offering contradictory advice. The true believers in each faith are openly scornful of anyone who hasn't bought into their version of the holy way to salvation. It's a religion, folks.

Here's the truth: there are no absolute and totally correct answers to many of the questions and dilemmas of diet and training. Blame Mother Nature because she's the one who dealt each of us a different hand of cards. Besides our genetic differences (can't do a thing about those), we differ in what kind of an environment we were brought up in (athletics encouraged or ignored), our financial freedom (if you don't need to work, you can train all day), our personalities, where we live (San Diego versus Alaska), what we do for a living (or what our parents do), whether the local grocery store stocks lots of healthy, fresh food or a lot of packaged junk, and an endless list of other variables.. There are hundreds of differences between each of every one of us and all of them affect how we respond to physical training.

These differences mean that we approach training from different perspectives with widely diverse levels of ability and trainability. All of these factors add up to—surprise!—wildly different results.

Toss in the fact that the medical and exercise sciences have yet to make up their collective mind about a lot of training and diet questions, and it's a wonder anybody ever gets into shape. The only totally honest claim you can make about any training plan is that it should work, most of the time, for most people. Absolute certainties are few and far between.

Enough convincing. Let's get started.

TWO-MINUTE BOARD

- Training is a life-long thing, not something you do just before the season starts.
- People are born lazy. You have to acknowledge that fact and learn how to work around it.
- Despite what you see on TV, there are no miracle diets, devices or pills that will make you fit with no effort.
- Working out is first and foremost . . . well, work.
- The fun part of working out is being in shape and putting those new muscles through their paces.
- No, this book won't make you a race winner all by itself.
- Fitness improvements don't happen in a straight line. It's more like climbing stairs.
- Get a complete physical before starting this or any other fitness program.

Chapter 2

THE BASICS OF TRAINING

For obvious reasons, this book has to fit the needs of a diverse audience, ranging from guys who've never so much as tripped over a dumbbell to the very fit gym rats and everybody in between. Even if you're a full-fledged work out junkie, take the time to read this chapter. The basics behind getting more fit and stronger have changed over the years and what you think you know may no longer be valid.

What Gets Trained?
Motocross and off-road riding is a subtle and complex sport that requires brute strength, cardiovascular endurance, balance, coordination, flexibility, and razor-edged reflexes to name a few of the obvious physical demands. There

Why train? With modern 450s putting out around 50 horsepower, you need to be in shape to control one of these ground-based moto-missles.

may be no other sport that's more difficult to train for because of the many factors involved.

In general terms, your training is in four areas:

Core Strength: Your core, central body musculature development. This is your foundation and getting your core into shape is necessary in order to follow a more comprehensive and focused training program.

Endurance: Unlike other sports, motocross doesn't have timeouts, yellow-flag pace laps, penalty shots, or teammates who can take up the slack. This makes non-stop endurance critical. It doesn't do you any good to be fast for two laps if the moto lasts five laps. Improving your cardiovascular (aerobic) endurance levels, besides making your heart and lungs stronger, helps your body develop a tolerance to lactic acid buildup in your muscles so you can keep on charging right through the last lap.

Muscular Strength: Controlling a motocross bike at speed requires substantial muscular strength, especially from your upper body—shoulders, arms, chest, and back. Nearly as important to bike control are the big muscles in your legs. In both cases, the goal isn't a bodybuilder's bulging muscles, but the type of muscular strength that's specific to racing a motorcycle. Being able to bench press 300 pounds may sound like a great training goal, but all that extra muscle will add up to dead weight that the bike has to haul around. The only time you really need to be able to bench press heavy weights is if you find yourself at the bottom of a pile of bikes in the first turn and need to get a motorcycle off your chest. At that point, it's probably not going to make much difference in your racing results.

Flexibility: Think of motocross as a high-speed ballet. If you watch Ricky Carmichael at speed, he's dancing all around the bike to keep it headed in the direction he wants. You need flexibility so your muscles can react quickly and smoothly to whatever the bike is doing or what you need it to do. Stiff, tight muscles are slow to react and easily injured.

Specific Training vs. Random Training

For sports training to produce results, it needs to be specific to the sport. Random training methods, even if they get you extremely fit, are only going to give you random results in your chosen sport. You don't want random results, you want specific accomplishments.

For training to produce the improvements you want, it has to contain these three elements:

Progression. Your body reacts to a stress situation (the work out), recovers, and adapts to that stress in the form of increased strength and endurance. This is the whole basis behind working out. You have to keep increasing the stress progressively to continuously challenge your muscles. If you apply the same workload week after week, you don't progress and you don't get any stronger. Lots of people train regularly yet complain of never seeing any improvement. The reason is there's no progression in their work outs. They do basically the same thing, time after time, with no increased stress. Their body has no reason to get stronger, so it doesn't.

Gradual Increase. The flip side to progressively tougher training is that if you add too much stress too quickly or with inadequate recovery, you'll overload your system and lose any performance gains. The rule, especially at the start of your training program, is to go slow. Too many people try to do too much, too fast. Trying to force your body to build itself up too quickly never works. The exception to this is the boot-camp approach, where you devote all of your time to training for weeks on end. Boot camps work, but it's rarely an option for most people, so give yourself permission to be patient and let your body adjust to the new stresses and get stronger in the way it prefers—gradually.

Adequate Rest. Contrary to what you might think, you don't build muscle while you're doing the exercise. When exercising, you're actually tearing the muscles down, not building them up. The building phase takes place only when you're resting. That's why you alternate between cardio work outs on one day that work one set of muscles, and strength training on the other day to work a different group of muscles. It's also why you have to make sure you're getting enough sleep, because that's when your body is at its busiest rebuilding. Work too hard without adequate recovery time and you'll end up burning out, getting injured, or seeing little or no progress.

There's a fourth element if you want your work out program to succeed: Keep track (quantify) of your training. You can't tell if you're making progress toward your goals if you don't keep a record. Your training plan (see Chapter 3) will give you a way to list your work outs, keep track of recovery time, and let you chart your progress. Without a training plan with quantified information, it's easy to fall into the trap of doing pretty much the same work out, day after day, and never getting better.

What are your numbers? Record them at right for later reference. You need to know where you're starting from before you can decide where to go with your training.

What Are Your Numbers?

You need to establish where you are right now in terms of fitness. Grab a pen and record the following information in the space at right:

Age: _____

Weight: _____

Height: _____

This is an optional section, but some people like having the information. Next, have someone measure your waist, upper arms, around your hips, and any other part of your body that you want to focus on during your training. In terms of fitness, the numbers don't mean anything, but if one of your goals is to drop a pants size, then it's important for you to know where you're starting from.

Waist (narrowest point of your midsection): _____

Abdomen (tape crosses over your belly button): _____

Hips (widest portion): _____

Chest: _____

Upper Arms (flexed): _____

Forearms (near the elbow): _____

Calves: _____

Next, tomorrow morning, when you wake up but before you get out of bed, take your pulse. This is your resting pulse rate and the most accurate time to do it is just after waking up, before you've dumped any caffeine into your bloodstream or done anything else that will affect the number. For better accuracy, you should do this three mornings in a row and then calculate your average.

Resting Pulse Rate: _____

Finally, surf over to www.fitwatch.com or another health and fitness website (see Chapter 9 for a list, but a little internet surfing will show you plenty more) and find out your Body Mass Index (BMI) and Basal Metabolism

Rate (BMR) numbers are. The BMI tells you whether your weight is normal or not, while the BMR tells you what your calorie needs are per day.

BMI: _____

BMR: _____

How Fit Are You?

Let's get a rough idea of where you're starting from. In racing terms, you want to find out if you're in the Novice, Intermediate, or Expert class as far as fitness goes. This information provides a starting point for designing a training program as detailed in the next chapter. Write your test results on page 20.

These tests are not a pass or fail type. No grades are being given. They provide a reference point so you can take stock of yourself now and refer back to the information later to see how much you've improved—or haven't. Since we're guys and we like to know how we compare to other guys, I've supplied typical good results for adult males in their twenties for these tests.

Upper-body strength: Find a sturdy bench or solid chairs and see how many dips you can do as a test of your upper body strength. As with all exercises, do it smoothly with proper form. Keep your back straight and ALL of the effort should be coming from your shoulders and upper arms.

Test: Chair Dips
Measures: Upper-Body Strength
You need a sturdy bench or armless chair. Sit on the bench with your heels on the floor, outstretched in front of you. Grasp the sides of the bench with your hands and inch off and away from the bench until you're supported by your heels and hands. Slowly lower yourself until your buttocks are close to touching the floor, hold for one second, and then push back up. Repeat as many times as you can.

Good Results: 10 dips

Your Score: _____

Test: Push-Ups to Failure
Measures: Muscular Endurance
Assume the pose (hands should be under the shoulders, no place else). Have someone lie on the floor in front of you, with their fist under your chest, thumb side up. That's your target (No helper? Put something about 4 or 5 inches tall to serve as a target). Do as many push-ups as you can until your arms turn to Jell-O.

Good Results: 40 push-ups

Your Score: _____

Test: 1.5-Mile Run
Measures: Aerobic Fitness
You need two things to do this test: A running track (a local high school or college) and enough aerobic fitness to run the distance. If you're not there yet in terms of fitness, start out with a walking program for a couple weeks first, then slowly upgrade it to a walk-jog routine. The typical 400 meter high school running track will give you 1.5 miles in six laps of running on the inside lane.

Good Results: 10 minutes or less

Your Score: _____

Test: Toe Touch
Measures: Flexibility
Sit on the floor, both legs straight in front of you. Reach forward as far as you can toward your toes.
Good Results: Wrist to toe

Your Score: _____

Test: Slow Sit-Up
Measures: Muscular Endurance
The usual bent-leg sit-up test involves seeing how many you can do in a minute. The problem is that most of us cheat like riverboat gamblers. The slow sit-up solves this problem by taking away all the opportunities to cheat. Lie on the floor with knees bent and feet flat on the floor. Extend your arms so they're out at your sides but off the floor, palms facing down. Sit up as slowly as possible, then return to the starting position as slowly as possible. Done properly, it's 5 seconds up and 5 seconds down.

For the aerobic endurance test you need a runner's watch so you can time yourself and . . .

Good Results: Five slow sit-ups in one minute (a lot of people can't even do one)

Your score: _____

Now, put a date on this page, next to your information above. Congratulations. This is your starting point. You can come back to this page as your training progresses and see the changes you've made.

The Training Mantra

I like to keep things simple. You should too. Life has enough built-in complexity.

Most of the training, diet, or lifestyle books out there are filled with so many rules that trying to follow the advice is impossible unless you have a photographic memory and enough patience to qualify for sainthood. Eventually you do something you shouldn't, eat something that's banned, or simply get weary of trying to remember which day of the diet/life/training plan you're supposed to be on. It's little wonder that most diet plans are doomed to failure and that most training programs quickly get to be a boring chore.

Since I was also frustrated at trying to make sense of it all, a number of years ago, I formulated a few simple rules about life, training, and staying in shape. I wanted something I could always remember, to help me steer my way through the maze of choices. The fewer the rules, the easier they are to remember and the harder they are to ignore. The rules I came up with are as follows:

1. Doing anything is better than doing nothing.
2. Everything counts.
3. Eat to win.
4. There is no off-season.

I won't claim that you'll find the answers to all of life's questions in those four bits of advice, but you'll come close. Whenever I'm trying to decide about a work out, a meal, how to spend my limited spare time, or any of the basic whatevers of life, I just refer to the rules above and usually find my answer.

Some explanation:

Doing Anything Is Better than Doing Nothing

If you want to get and stay in shape, then start to think of the whole world as your gym and every waking hour as the time you have available. Choosing to do something—*anything*—active instead of slouching on the sofa in front of the boob tube pays off big. Don't have a full hour to work out? Then spend 30 minutes of the time you do have. Take your dog for a walk, ride your bicycle, go for a quick run around the block, shoot some hoops in the driveway . . . it doesn't matter what you do so much as being active and burning calories. Everything you do, however minor it may seem at the time, contributes in some small way to your overall physical well-being.

Assuming you spend 8 hours a day asleep, that leaves 16 hours with your eyes open and the ability to make some decisions about how to spend every one of those 960 minutes. Your goal throughout your life is to fill the maximum number of those minutes with activity of some type. It can be as simple as taking the stairs to your office, parking your car a little further away from the grocery store, or as complex as an exhausting circuit training routine in the gym. Everybody has the same number of hours available every day. It's how you put them to use that creates the differences between us.

. . . and a local high school or college running track. Be sure to warm-up and drink some water before your test run. Run in the inside lane for 1.5 miles (6 laps) and record your time from your stopwatch. Do the whole 6 laps, even if you have to walk some of it or slow down to a weary trot, because your time will tell you about your aerobic fitness.

Everything Counts

Everything you do, including turning the pages of this book, requires energy and consumes some calories. Calories are simply a unit of energy and not some evil ingredient in food. You want to balance your caloric intake with your caloric consumption, or your body saves it for you as fat. Everything you do, everything you consume, contributes toward that daily caloric balance. Your job is to keep burning calories so they never have a chance to become excess flab.

Can't decide between helping yourself to a glazed donut at a meeting or munching on an apple? Remember, *everything counts*. Yeah, you'll probably work it off—or some of it anyhow—when you get to the gym, but would you rather be sweating off 250 calories of donut or 90 calories of apple? Do the math.

If you like keeping track in minute detail of what you eat and drink, use a food diary (see Chapter 5) to record the calorie numbers alongside your training plan. It's well worth the effort because the numbers will surprise you. Doing a little research and increasing your knowledge will help you make intelligent decisions.

Eat to Win

The American diet is a health disaster of yet unrealized proportions. It may ultimately end up being more deadly and affecting more people than smoking. Your job is to eat a healthy mix of high-quality foods that benefit your training goals and overall health, while sidestepping all the foodie landmines so cunningly spread in your path.

Diet should be a noun, not a verb in your vocabulary. You should be the one making the decisions about what you eat and in what quantity—not your parents, your spouse, your kids, and certainly not some advertising agency pimping for a restaurant chain. It's your life and your training plan, so you should be deciding whether you really need that double cheeseburger with bacon.

Be sure to read Chapter 5: Eating to Win for more details.

There Is No Off-Season

Sports have off-seasons; your body doesn't. Staying in shape should be a lifetime commitment. It's much easier to adopt and stick to a training plan and healthy eating habits if you think in this way. Off-seasons provide excuses to fall back into unhealthy habits and get out of shape.

From every way you can look at things, it's better to stay in shape year-round and to adjust your training to peak for certain periods (important races or the meat of the race season) than to yo-yo back and forth between training and trying to get back into shape. Instead of spending your training time losing the extra pounds you gained in the off-season and reacquiring the muscles and endurance you had earlier, your goal is to never lose it and never have to get it back.

The Health Club

While it's possible to build a pretty strong body without any equipment at all (martial arts schools are experts at doing exactly this), most people will need access to a variety of work out equipment. Your choices are to rent it by joining a health club or buy it and use it at home. Either choice has some tradeoffs.

Health clubs offer the most equipment and it's usually far better gear than anything you can afford—or have room for—in your home gym. There are other advantages, such as classes and sports leagues, to add variety to your training, a chance to socialize (which can be both good and bad), a pool for low-impact water training (great when recovering from injuries), personal trainers to turn to for advice, juice bars, hot tubs, and the overall convenience of one-stop, do-everything workout headquarters.

The downside, of course, is the cost, contracts, having to share and wait for equipment to be free, a workout

Touching your toes is a measure of flexibility. Sit on the floor, legs in front of you, and reach forward toward your toes as far as you can. You're pretty flexible if you can stretch far enough so that your wrists touch your toes and not bad if you can touch them with your fingertips.

Getting, and more important staying, fit and healthy is really pretty simple. Just be sure you do something active every single day. An easy run in the evening, with attractive scenery, in-line skating, or even walking the dog (and Fido probably needs the exercise, too) is all it takes.

for equipment to be free, a workout culture that might be at odds with your goals, too many chances to socialize, too many training alternatives, too many distractions, the drive, parking hassles, hidden fees, and all the other joys of communal life. The right gym can be a major boost to your training and the wrong one will make you wish you'd never seen the place.

Finding the right gym takes research. Do this when evaluating them:

• Visit several that are conveniently located either near your daily commute route or your home.

• Visit at the time(s) when you're most likely to work out to see how crowded it is at that time.

• Talk to other members; ask how they like it, how long they've been

members, and if there are any negatives.

• What's the culture like? Are the free weights monopolized by giant muscled creatures who only vaguely look human? Is it predominantly female and the focus is on the latest aerobic fad class?

• Is there a contract and what does it include and not include?

• Are the hours convenient for you, including weekends? Some gyms are geared strictly for the downtown business set and others are suburban country clubs.

• Ask about a trial membership or trial work out visit. In most areas, it's a buyer's market (that's you) so don't be rushed into signing a contract. Ask about special prices for family or buddy memberships.

• Is the locker room clean, dry, and you don't think you'll pick up any new diseases by walking through it?

• For your cardio work outs, is there a good place nearby (a park, trails, good neighborhood) so you can happily do your sweating outdoors?

• Do they have enough equipment and the right kind for your training? The best clubs will have both a good selection of free weights as well as the muscle-building machines.

The Home Gym

There are a lot of advantages to keeping your work outs on the home front, the biggest being convenience. There are no driving or parking hassles; no waiting to use a piece of equipment; no blaring music other than your own choices; all the gear is set up for you personally so you don't have to waste time adjusting the seat or weight stack; and beyond buying the equipment,

there's no added cost.

The flip side is that the no-drive convenience of working out at home comes at a price. Unless you have an exceptionally large house, finding space for your workout equipment can be a major challenge. Basements, spare bedrooms, or garages are the usual choices, and then you have to deal with low ceilings, musty smells, and limited space. Few people can afford professional workout machines comparable to what's found in any health club, and equipment geared for home use tends to be less durable.

Let's not forget that a man's home is his hassle. Houses were invented to make sure you don't have any spare time. Something always needs fixing, mowing, or painting. It can be hard to be as selfish as you must be to get your work outs done when you're looking at the uncut lawn and the dangling gutter. Then there are the added distractions of family, a ringing phone, unanswered email, and the work or homework piled up on your desk. As distracting as the cute person in the tight spandex outfit might be at the health club, she's nothing compared to the distractions of home life.

The Racer's $200 Home Gym

The myth is that you need to either belong to a health club where there's tons of equipment or invest a couple thousand dollars in a home gym set-up as seen on TV.

Let's consider a third alternative—a little of both: a club membership plus a couple hundred dollars spent on home gym gear that you can put to good and regular use. For the big stuff, never buy it new. Barely-been-sweated-

---

MIND GAMES

Having a hard time getting your sorry butt out the door for a run or bicycle ride? Just tell yourself you're only going to go a couple of easy miles. Once you're in motion, tell yourself another lie to get yourself to do *just* another mile . . . and another and so on. Your muscles want to work out; it's your brain that wants to stay indoors and eat Cheez-Whiz while watching Oprah.

Buy or build a chin-up bar for your house. A lot of gyms no longer have this essential piece of training gear, so put one in your house and use it.

prices is easier to find than hungry mosquitoes in a swamp. Every December and January, people buy new work out machines, determined to lose the holiday pounds and start the new year in a sleek, new body. By February, 90 percent of it is gathering dust. By April, it's up for sale in the classifieds or garage sales.

Some places to look for bargains:

• www.craigslist.com is a web site justifiably famous for having some interesting bargains. You may even find what you need for free. All you have to do is pick it up.

• Garage sales, especially multi-family or neighborhood sales events will almost always produce at least one weight bench and a set of weights.

• Goodwill and other donation stores are usually the destination for the stuff that didn't get sold at the garage sales.

• Sitting on the curb waiting for trash pick-up.

• Moving sales.

• Classified ads in your local paper.

• Flea markets.

• www.eBay.com, www.overstock.com, and other online auction sites can be great resources (but beware of shipping charges).

Here's what you need and what you should expect to pay:

• Adjustable weight-lifting bench with an adjustable rest for the barbell. Make sure it's wide enough and long enough for you. Some of them are so skinny or short that your back won't have adequate support. ($20 to $50 used)

• A set of dumbbells in a variety of weights. Best are the one-piece versions as you're more likely to use them if you don't have to play around with changing weight plates. You'll also train more efficiently if you don't have to pause while changing plates. ($20 to $50 used)

• A set of weight plates for the barbell. You want a set of weights that give you a wide range to work with. So you want 5-, 10-, 15-, and 20-lb sets. ($20 to $50 used)

• A cut-off broom handle or closet bar, a piece of rope, and a 5-lb weight. ($0)

• A rubber mat long enough to lie on. (free to $20)

• A good adult-size jump rope. ($6)

• An exercise (a.k.a: Swiss or stability) ball—those big ones used for exercises. ($20 to $40)

• Chin-up bar that screws into a doorway. ($15 to $25; buy this new)

Optional, but good to have, items include medicine balls in various weights, a stand for the weight plates and dumbbells, something you can

punch (a heavy bag, not the speed bag), and a preacher's bar for bicep curls.

With a little shopping, scrounging, haggling, luck, and persistence, you can outfit your home gym for $100 to $200. You'll have the essentials for most strength training routines for less than the cost of a race weekend.

For things like an exercise mat and jump rope, you can find good quality gear at very reasonable prices in common discount stores like Target, CostCo, Meijers, and K-Mart. There's no need to go to a sporting goods store and pay inflated prices for these basics.

Chapter 3

DESIGNING YOUR PERSONAL TRAINING PLAN

If you want something done right, you have to do it yourself. With training plans, there's no truer statement.

For training to have lasting, predictable, and measurable effects, you need a plan. Trying to train without a plan and a method to measure your progress is like trying to read a book with randomly numbered pages. It won't tell you what you need to know.

It's an impossible task for me or anyone else to come up with a perfect training plan for you. Each of us is unique and starting from different places in terms of age, size, natural ability, and everything else right down to shoe size and tolerance for pain. Training plans that have real value simply don't come in a one-size-fits-all format. I can make a plan for myself because I know all about me, but it's close to impossible to create a useful training plan for someone you don't know, can't see, and can't talk to.

Here's an example: I'm tall, naturally lean, and much stronger than I look (damn, I hate that) because my muscles are geared more for endurance than weightlifter bulkiness. I'm also stubborn and able to push myself to the point of exhaustion, both of which are good things for running marathons, riding enduros, or doing multiple motos on a 100-degree day. If I were shorter, taller, heavier, lighter, less stubborn, more flexible, or bulkier, the sports I like and the way I train would be different. A training program that works the

Your personal training plan starts here.

Start by listing your training goals. Goals need to be specific to be attainable.

best for me is not necessarily going to work as well for you. All the exercise gurus want you to believe that if something works for them, it automatically has to work for everybody else. That's just not true.

If a training program isn't tailored to the one person actually doing the work, it's not going to be much good. A training plan has to fit who you are, your physique, level of fitness, commitment, willingness to work, and the results you want. A personal training plan should always emphasize the "personal" part.

Training Log or Training Plan?

Just to ease the confusion, a training *plan* and a training *log* are totally different things, but you use them together.

The *training plan* is what you intend to accomplish. It's your work out schedule for an 8- to 12-week period. You establish specific goals (amount of weight loss, distance run, level of fitness, etc.) and then formulate a plan that will get you there.

The *training log* is your day-to-day record of what you actually did during your work outs in pursuit of your training plan. The training log is optional, although highly recommended. It's your map of how you got from here (your current level of fitness) to there (the kind of shape you want to be in).

The Man with a Plan

Ignore those TV infomercials touting miracle muscle-building gadgets. The real miracle work out device is a notebook, a pen, and a calendar.

Even if you somehow got a copy of Ricky Carmichael's personal training plan, it wouldn't do you much good because he's in better shape than 99.99 percent of the world's population. To have any value, a training plan must be a highly personalized document that balances your goals against your abilities, weaknesses, strengths, and daily schedule.

A training plan forces you to focus on what's important, reminds you of your goals big and small, helps you chart your progress and—most importantly—prevents you from wasting time. Because you have way too many things going on in your life, making full

use of the little spare time you have available for your training is critical. A full-time athlete or pro rider can goof off a bit, or experiment with some new training ideas that may or may not work, without sacrificing much in terms of results because it's such a small amount of time out of a big chunk. You don't have that option. You need to put every minute of those precious spare hours in their proper place and perspective. Time is not on your side, dude.

Questions to Ask Yourself

Get a notebook and pen or use the examples shown here. You need to write answers to some questions, so don't just skim through this without doing the writing. Think about your answers because the sooner you crank out your training plan, the sooner you can start to make good things happen.

When answering these questions, list specific, measurable goals: Times, dates, weight, race wins, waist size, bicep size, whatever specifics will give you concrete guideposts for how you're doing. Avoid generalities like "be stronger." Stronger where and stronger how? Pinpoint your goals, but realize you're not engraving them in stone. You can always change your plan and your goals later, as your training progresses and you learn what works for you and what doesn't.

The questions you have to answer for yourself are these:

1. What are my top three training goals? Some possibilities are to lose a specific amount of weight, have better endurance as measured by total distance run or bicycled, stronger arms as measured by number of push-ups, and so on.
Goal 1: _____
Goal 2: _____
Goal 3: _____

2. Where do I need the most improvement? Make a decision about the one area you need the most improvement. Maybe it's endurance? Upper body strength? Weight loss? By choosing one primary goal, you can focus on that goal on the days when you

MORE SPEED

Bored with the same old work outs? Enter a local competitive event—a running race, bicycle race, etc. Not only can you count the event as part of your weekly training, the crowd and the competition will likely produce a hard work out and a faster time than if you were just doing your usual routine. There's nothing like having someone challenging you for a sprint to the finish line to get the adrenaline pumping and the legs a'churning.

only have enough time to do one short work out.

3. What bad habits are holding me back that I need to change? Eating or drinking too much? No work outs at all? Daily stops at the donut shop? Put them on paper as a first step to changing them.

4. What kind of shape am I really in? Be honest. Poor, mediocre, okay, good, or excellent? Give yourself an honest evaluation based on the tests you took in Chapter 2 (you did take them, didn't you? If not, go back and find out what your numbers are. Enter them in the chart below for reference in creating your training plan.

5. Look at your schedule and figure out where you can make an appointment with yourself for at least five total hours a week. Five hours a week should be your barest of bare minimums, with ten hours being more realistic if you want to see quicker and better results. This is five or ten hours spread out over the week, not crammed into the weekend, and it doesn't include racing or riding time. Make an appointment with yourself to train, putting it on the calendar like any other appointment. You don't "find" the time to train, you "make" it. Just figure out what other time commitments or appointments

you can choose to skip. For example, stuff like the post-work bull and beer sessions, channel surfing, video games, and other time-eaters. Watch TV at the health club instead.

NUMBER OF HOURS I'LL TRAIN PER WEEK AND WHEN

Monday: _____
Tuesday: _____
Wednesday: _____
Thursday: _____
Friday: _____
Saturday: _____
Sunday: _____

---

6. Finally, list one or two short-term goals for a month in the future. You want a short-term goal as a target to shoot at and a way to stay motivated. It's hard to stay motivated for months on end chasing a too-distant objective. Again, it's got to be specific, such as a quicker time in the 1.5-mile run, an amount of weight lost, sit-ups done, or even something as simple as not missing any scheduled work outs for a month.

GOALS

Short Term Goal # 1: _____
Short Term Goal # 2: _____

Now What?
You've now got a very complete summary of your training plan. You've identified what you need to work on, what your goals are, and how much time you're going to devote each week to training. All that's left to do is to fill in the blanks and go to work.

See the Appendix for a training plan form you can copy as a starting point, or create something of your own design. Make some copies and put them where you can refer to your plan easily—your office wall, on your computer monitor, or in your daily planner.

FITNESS EVALUATION

Resting Pulse
Time in 1.5-mile run: _____
    minutes: _____
Push-ups to Failure: _____

Sit-Up Test
Dip Test: _____
Flexibility: _____
    Good _____
    So-so _____
    Stiff as a steel rod _____
BMI: _____
BMR: _____
Waist (narrowest point of your midsection): _____
Abdomen (tape crosses over your belly button): _____
Hips (widest portion): _____
Chest: _____
Upper Arms (flexed): _____
Forearms (near the elbow): _____
Calves: _____

It's now okay to jump ahead and read the chapters that deal with the things you want to focus on. For example, Chapter 5 covers weight loss/control; Chapter 6 focuses on endurance (also called aerobic and cardiovascular) conditioning, an area where almost everyone needs to put in some time; Chapter 7 is all about building strength for motocross; and so on. Use the sample Work out Plan in the Appendix, combined with the corresponding chapters to design your personal plan. Or just start with a blank piece of paper and simply write it out.

Here's an example of my work out plans for two days in a typical week. My usual routine has me doing my strength training Monday-Wednesday-Friday and sandwich in three distance runs on Tuesday-Thursday and Saturday. Don't be either put off or too impressed with my work out. It's a list of what I plan to do, but may not actually accomplish. I sometimes have to surrender to the same lame excuses all of us can come up with. Even though there are some days I can't follow my plan for one reason or another, at least I start each week knowing what I'm going to be doing.

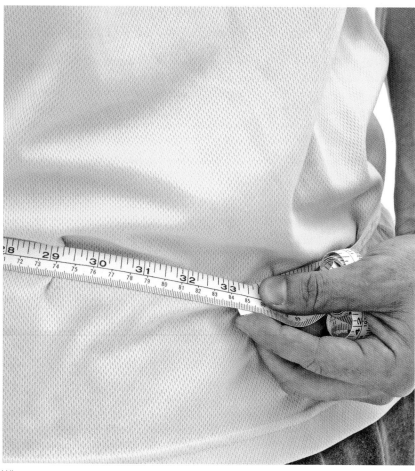

What are your numbers? If you didn't do the tests from Chapter 2, do them now. You need to know where you're starting from.

MONDAY

Warm-Up:

Crunches	2 sets of 100, different positions
Dumbbell fly	10 reps, 2 sets, 20 lbs
Superman	10 reps
Push-ups	20 regular
	10 on exercise ball
	10 slow

Weight:

Lat pull-downs	3 sets, 6-8 reps, 150 lbs
Lat cable pull-ups	3 sets, 6 reps, 140 lbs
Cable pull-overs	3 sets, 6-8 reps, 80 lbs
Cable Woodcutters	4 sets, 2 each side, 10 reps, 110 lbs
Row	4 sets, 6-8 reps, 185 lbs
Hamstring machine	3 sets, 10 reps, 125 lbs
Quads machine	3 sets, 10 reps, 155 lbs
Hammer curls	2 sets, 6-8 reps, w/dumbbells 40lb left/45 lb right

Cool-Down:

Wall sit	1 minute
Eagle stretch	
Calf raises	

TUESDAY

Warm-Up:

Push-ups	20 regular

Cardio:

Hill running route	7 miles

Cool-Down:

Achilles stretch	
Groin stretch	
Dips in park	4 sets of 10

WEDNESDAY

Repeat of Monday's work out

Creating a Training Log

You can't tell where you're going without knowing where you've been. I confess to being a big fan of keeping a training log because it helps to keep you focused. Once you get into the ritual of filling in that day's work out information, the need to record something for that day can be enough motivation to head out the door and get your work out done. Think of your training log as a bargain-bin time travel machine. It lets you revisit past work outs, note significant facts about your current training, show your progress toward your goals, and plan ahead for the future.

Keeping a training log is a lot like any other aspect of training: you've got to teach yourself to do it and then keep on doing it every day. It's a responsibility you set for yourself if you're serious about your training. A log is a training tool, and it's every bit as important as a set of barbells and weights.

Need more convincing? A work out log does this:

• Keeps you focused on your goals.

• Shows your improvement over time, something that's otherwise hard to verify.

• Gives you an attainable goal to meet each day (just fill in that day's work out).

• Teaches you what you're doing right and what went wrong by giving you a capsule view of what you were doing last week, last month, last year.

• Helps keep your diet healthy. There's nothing more humbling than recording a pizza-n-beer binge on paper, and then noting your next day's performance disaster.

• Gives you a place to record all those Great Thoughts you get while working out—and yes, exercise has been proven to be a great way to find solutions to various job and life problems.

• Motivates you to train harder. Your training log keeps you from wimping out.

• Lets you plan ahead for important races, work outs, and fitness goals. No more looking at the calendar and realizing your biggest race of the season is a week away and you've done diddly-squat.

TRAIN WHILE SICK!

Should you try to suck it up and train while sick? You're sniffy, sneezy, queasy, maybe with a fever and definitely out of sorts. Common sense (and most Moms) say it's best to stay in bed and get better, but that's not always the right choice or the one you prefer when you've got a training program that you're dedicated to.

Here are some guidelines, and that's all they are, because you have to make the decision for yourself based on how you feel and how you react when sick. Don't attempt any personal bests and consider your scheduled work out as a success just for getting it done. Don't overdo your work out because that can delay your recovery even more. It is always best to err on the side of caution.

SYMPTOMS!

If you're sniffling but not achy or feverish, it's probably allergies, so go work out (yeah!). You'll feel better afterward. Really.

Sniffling, achy, tired, and feverish all at the same time? You've got a cold or the flu, so stay home from work (you're contagious) and recover. Get a lot of rest and watch all those taped Supercross races you've got stashed away. Forget about working out.

Chills or sweats? Sounds like a fever, so get the thermometer and confirm. Fevers are a free Get Out of Work/School card. Stay home because you're probably contagious with the flu or a cold. Rest a lot, drink plenty of fluids, and bag the work out.

Fever with white spots on your tonsils? Get to a doctor because it may be strep throat. Of course, you're not going to work or the gym because you are contagious.

Coughing? If it's a tickle or feels like postnasal drip, it's either a cold or allergies. If there aren't any other cold symptoms or fever, you can work out if you want. If, however, your cough is deep, brings up green mucus, or leaves you short of breath, see a doctor. It could just be a cold, but it could also be pneumonia, a sinus infection, or bronchitis. No work out.

Sinus pain? Pain around the eyes, top of your forehead, or cheekbones are signs of a sinus infection but it could also be a bad cold. Call in sick, go see a doctor, and skip the work out.

Upset stomach? Nausea, vomiting, diarrhea, and aches, especially if accompanied by fever, are all signs you need to do four things: 1. See a doctor; 2. Stay home; 3. Don't even think about working out; 4. Drink a lot of fluids. The rule of thumb is that if you can hold down food, even if you sometimes feel nauseous, then you can go to work . . . and maybe even work out.

Headache? Head pain can be caused by the common cold or a variety of other illnesses. However, if you can't tolerate noise or light, you probably have a migraine and should skip everything to curl up in bed. A mild headache, however, often goes away in the course of working out. Only use a headache as an excuse to call in sick if it's severe or comes with other symptoms.

Achy, tired, feeling listless? It might be early signs of some bug, or it may be just the daily strain of work and life in general. Go for a run or bicycle or engage in some other aerobic work out that gets the blood moving and your lungs flapping. Odds are you'll finish the work out feeling refreshed and with none of that listlessness left.

How you use the training log is less important than simply using it. At first it may be a chore, but let's face it—a lot of what's involved in training is going to require discipline and a certain tolerance for boring chores you'd rather avoid. Some guidelines:

• Record your running or bicycle routes. You might discover your regular route is part of why you're not seeing any

You can't tell where you're going and how you're doing without knowing where you started. That's why it's important to keep a training log. You can buy a variety of training logs at the bookstore, or you can create your own with a workbook and pen.

Some people prefer to use their planner calendar to record their training as well as schedule work outs.

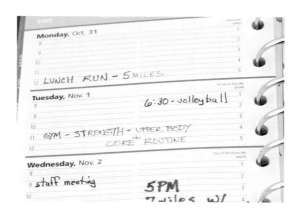

• Cross-training can be anything that is physical. Mowed the lawn using a push mower? Played two hours of sand-pit volleyball with the guys? An hour of martial arts at your karate school?

• How you feel: This is an anything goes category. Got some injuries? Had a sleepless night because your teenager was out on a date? Big party with too much food and drink? Feeling punky and suspect you're coming down with something? Here's where you record it all.

• Thoughts/Comments: These days my work outs are usually solo, which means I get to spend a lot of time inside my head. Solitude combined with exertion does magical things to your brain. Problems that you'd been trying to resolve at work or home with zero success, suddenly jell into solutions. Write them down here.

• Put pictures in your log. Digital cameras make this easy to do. Maybe some before-and-after shots of yourself from when you started training and the remarkably skinnier/stronger/faster new you? Or from races, trophy in hand; with your buddies during a marathon bench-racing session; that new bike you want to buy. Anything that will help to keep you motivated.

• READ your log. That's what it's there for. It's a tool to help you learn things about your training routines, what's working and what isn't, and change the plan as needed. Plus notes about things like what pair of running shoes you loved and which ones ate your toes for lunch can be very useful.

Sample Training Log
You can purchase printed training logs at the bookstore, create your own on your computer, download versions from various online sources, or copy the version here.

improvement. It could be too flat, too long, too short, or too mind-numbingly boring to keep you motivated. Doing the exact same training route every time leads to staleness.

• Record either distance or time or both for your endurance work outs, whichever you prefer. Me, I always like to know the mileage of what I've been doing as the time aspect doesn't usually tell me anything. I can run fast or I can run slow and use up the same amount of time either way, but I'll be doing vastly different distances.

WEEK _____ Week of _____ to _____

Upcoming Race(s): _____

MONDAY
Route: _____
Distance/Time: _____
Weight Training: _____
Cross-Training: _____
How I feel: _____
Thoughts/Comments: _____

TUESDAY
Route: _____
Distance/Time: _____
Weight Training: _____
Cross-Training: _____
How I feel: _____
Thoughts/Comments: _____

WEDNESDAY
Route: _____
Distance/Time: _____
Weight Training: _____
Cross-Training: _____
How I feel: _____
Thoughts/Comments: _____

THURSDAY
Route: _____
Distance/Time: _____
Weight Training: _____
Cross-Training: _____
How I feel: _____
Thoughts/Comments: _____

FRIDAY
Route: _____
Distance/Time: _____
Weight Training: _____
Cross-Training: _____
How I feel: _____
Thoughts/Comments: _____

SATURDAY
Route: _____
Distance/Time: _____
Weight Training: _____
Cross-Training: _____
How I feel: _____
Thoughts/Comments: _____

SUNDAY
Route: _____
Distance/Time: _____
Weight Training: _____
Cross-Training: _____
How I feel: _____
Thoughts/Comments: _____

WEEKLY TOTALS:

RUN/BIKE TOTALS TO DATE:

TWO-MINUTE BOARD

- The only person who can design a training plan that will work for you is you.
- A training *plan* tells you where you're going; a training *log* tells you where you've been. You need both.
- If you didn't do the fitness tests from Chapter 2, this is your second chance to gather the information.
- The miracle training device you never see sold on TV is this: a notebook, a pen, a calendar, and some times spent thinking about your goals.

Chapter 4

CORE TRAINING

Your body has about 650 muscles and if you check the bookstores, it seems like there's a work out or exercise video for each and every one of them.

Fortunately, racers only need to focus on a few of them: shoulders, upper and lower back, forearms, quads, hamstrings, chest, upper arms, and let's not forget the most important muscle of all, your heart. Still, while the list is a bit long, fortunately the exercises listed here work all of them in groups.

In case you've been thumbing through this book looking for the meaty portions, this is where you start. You're probably anxious to kick-start your training and to collect on those promises of more strength and endurance. If you still need convincing, go re-read Chapter 2; otherwise, this is your personal starting line, right here.

Let me tell you a secret: If you only did the core exercises in this chapter plus some of the aerobic training explained in Chapter 6, you'd be so far ahead of most people in terms of conditioning that it would be no contest. In a sense, you only need these two chapters to develop one strongly conditioned body.

There are some well-publicized training programs out there that try to trademark the name "core" as if it's some special and unique type of training that only those coaches were smart enough to devise. That's just one more of those training-as-religion things.

Core training in the generic sense is making sure your back, chest, and abdominal muscles—your body's core—are strong enough to support and power the rest of the body. Think of core training as the foundation for any type of physical activity, whether it's racing a motorcycle or playing volleyball. Core exercises should always be a part of your training, even if you don't do anything else. They also make a good warm-up routine.

Most of these exercises will be very familiar since you probably first learned and attempted them in your school PE classes. These are exercises you should never stop doing for one very good reason: They deliver the goods.

A strong core is the foundation you build your training—and racing—upon.

All-Natural Work Outs

Despite the claims of TV ads and popular myth, you don't need a fully equipped health club or lavish home gym. You can do an amazingly thorough job building strength by using nothing more than gravity and your body. Martial arts schools traditionally have little of the normal gym equipment you might expect. Instead, these schools teach their students to use their body weight and sometimes the weight of their fellow students to develop the necessary muscle and bulk. There's a lot of wisdom in this.

Practicing these core exercises gives you a portable gym, good for travel to any country, requiring no more suitcase room than a pair of gym shorts and shirt. If you don't think you can get stronger without a lot of gear to play with, prepare to be disappointed. Bodyweight training should be your starting point for any type of work out.

Do This First

In case you did actually start reading here, I'll repeat an earlier bit of advice and warning: Before starting any physical training program, get a complete physical exam performed by your doctor. You're going to be pushing your body hard and your doctor can tell you whether it's up to it or not. If you're male, you're probably also good at skipping doctor's appointments. Don't do that! One reason women live longer than men is because they go to the doctor more often.

Warming Up

Just as you have to put the choke on to start your bike and allow it to warm up, your body needs the same consideration. Muscles perform better and are less likely to pull or strain when they're gradually brought up to speed.

• A warm-up should be about 5 to 10 minutes of activity that gets some sweat popping out of your forehead and your heart rate accelerating. It shouldn't be so long or so intense that you wear yourself out before you've actually begun your training, nor so easy that

there's no effort involved. Do one of these warm-ups:

• Jump rope. Besides getting your heart ticking over faster, it helps your balance, reflexes, and coordination. Jumping rope may be the best warm-up for most people, most times. (See the sidebar for a way to make this even more challenging.)

• Five minutes of easy running, starting slow and increasing to a moderate but still gentle pace.

• Five to ten minutes on a stationary bicycle or elliptical trainer at a light difficulty level.

• Five to ten minutes of climbing stairs. You can do this almost anywhere.

• Ten minutes of doing basic core exercises such as push-ups, sit-ups, or crunches.

As you become more fit, your warm-ups will have to become a little tougher and last longer. Thanks to decades of running, my cardiovascular level is pretty high so a warm-up for me usually involves 15 minutes on a stationary bike or 15 minutes of crunches, push-ups, and jumping rope. By the time you need to stretch out your warm-ups, you'll know it's necessary just from becoming attuned to your body's fitness signals.

NOT JUST FOR KIDS

Rope jumping is one of the most effective warm-ups and fat-burning exercises you can do. When you get tired of jumping rope in the traditional way, try this: Instead of holding the rope handles palm up, grab them so your palms are down with your thumbs facing in. This minor change takes the wrists out of the picture and forces the muscles of your upper back and shoulders to spin the rope. Yes, it's tougher. That's the whole point.

Start your core exercise routine by warming up. Jumping rope for five minutes is a great way to do this because it also wakes up your reflexes and timing while providing a cardio boost.

Race Day Warm-Ups

Warming up isn't just for when you're training. It should be a part of your race day strategy as well. If you watch elite runners before the start of a race, you'll see all of them doing quick sprints away from the start line, then jogging back. During Lance Armstrong's seven conquests of the Tour de France, he would spend 30 minutes on a stationary bike, just before he attacked the max-effort time trials, racing against the clock. Warm-ups prepare the body to work at maximum capacity.

For a motorcycle racer, one way to warm up before a race is to do some quick push-ups and stretches as shown in Chapter 10. You're not trying to wear yourself out, you just want to send a wakeup call to your muscles.

Going to the start line without warming up means that you'll be spending the first lap fighting cold, stiff, creaky, and easily injured muscles.

To Stretch or Not to Stretch?

Stretching is not the same as warming up. Stretches usually don't kick your heart rate up much, if at all. While some people swear by pre-work out stretches as a way to prevent injuries, others swear at it as the cause of those same strains. Scientific studies tend to muddle things. Some say stretching makes a difference and others find exactly the opposite. The current generally accepted advice is that the best time to stretch is *after* your exercise session, as part of your cool-down.

My advice and experience is that stretching is one of those things where you need to experiment and discover what works best for you. If you do a dedicated warm-up as described above, you've also stretched. Stretching is a personal thing that depends on how each individual reacts. For some sports—karate, for example—I stretch religiously in preparation. For other sports, such as running, I don't stretch unless I'm entered in a race and need to go fast right from the gun. It's what works for me based on years of experi-ence. You need to experiment and find out what works for you.

One time you absolutely should stretch, however, is just before practice at the track. Your muscles are cold and tight then, so loosen up first. Practice is one of the most stressful periods of the day. You are battling to find out where the track goes, while dodging the 200 other riders intent on winning practice. Stretching just before your practice session will let you focus on practicing, not collecting strains and muscle pulls.

A Core Exercise Routine

Core exercises should be a part of every work out since they help build the muscular foundation for everything else you're trying to do. Perform a variety of these exercises or their variations. It can be a work out itself or just a good warm-up. Most of these require no equipment, but I believe everyone should have and use a chin-up bar and an exercise ball (also called a Swiss ball, stability ball, etc.).

Each exercise targets a group of muscles. Do all or most of these core exercises for every work out.

Push-Ups: Push-ups are a cliché and a staple of every military movie ever made. Yell "drop and give me twenty" and everybody knows what you're talking about. The basic gym class push-up is still the go-to guy for building chest muscles, but you should also try the variations shown in the sidebar. A push-up begins with your back straight, your hands positioned slightly wider than shoulder width apart, and your legs balance on your toes. Lower yourself steadily until your nose touches the floor, then push yourself back up. Be smooth, not jerky. Your back will have to slightly arch as you lower yourself, but only a little bit, and not into a major curve.

Modified Push-Up: A modified push-up is for when you can't do a regular push-up. It'll help you build some muscle so you can advance to doing the regular version. You still have to display proper form: back straight, ankles crossed and tucked up by your butt so your weight is on your thighs and not your kneecaps.

Push Up

Drop and give me 20! Push-ups may be a cliché, but that's because they work. Stronger shoulders and arms of steel are what you get in exchange. Proper form is: place your arms under your shoulders, back just very slightly arched, balance on your toes, and go ALL the way down in a smooth motion. Your head never moves, so don't think you're doing a real pushup if you look like a bobble-head doll.

PUSH-UP VARIATIONS

Are regular push-ups getting too easy for you? Try these variations:

1. Raised-Leg Push-up: With your feet on a bench, exercise ball, stairs, or similar object, perform the push-up. The higher your feet, the tougher the push-up is to do.

2. Fingertip Push-Ups: Spread your fingers wide to create a bridge. Great for increasing finger strength.

3. Diamond Push-Up: Put your palms together flat on the floor, with the thumbs and index finger spread out to form a diamond. This really works the forearms and triceps.

4. Knife Hand Push-Up: Place your palms on the floor so that only the edges of the palms (little fingers down) are touching.

5. Wide-Track Push-Ups: Instead of having your hands placed beneath your shoulders, move them further out.

6. Slow Burn Push-Up: Start a regular push-up, lowering your body, but stop when your nose touches the floor and hold it there for a count of five. Then finish the upward motion. Your arms will be trembling after only a few of these, if you're doing them properly.

7. Springboard or Plyometric Push-Up: A standard push-up, but done with a lot more force and speed so that your palms come up off the floor, propelling your body upward. Then your arms come back down, catching and slowing your body as you return to the start position. Some people like to throw in a clap while their hands are off the floor, but you might want to get used to this exercise before risking that.

Don't limit your core routine to only in the gym. If you're running through a park on your endurance work out, and there are sturdy benches or picnic tables nearby, stop and do a quick set of push-ups. These park benches are spaced about 100 yards apart on my main running route, and my usual routine is to stop at each one and alternate between push-ups and dips as I run from bench to bench. It provides a change of pace while also adding some strength work to my run.

Modified Push-Up

If you can't yet do a real pushup yet, do the modified version with your knees on the floor. Modified pushups over time will get you to the point where you can do the proper version.

CRUNCH VARIATIONS

The standard crunch has gotten boring? Well, learn to suffer in new ways with any of the following variations.

Raised Legs: Both legs, ankles crossed, held in midair while you do a standard crunch.

Frog Leg Crunch: Feet on the floor and legs spread in a "V." This one you'll feel in your groin muscles as well as your abs.

One Leg Up: One leg held in midair, the other planted on the floor. Do a set and then switch legs.

Crunches: Call 'em sit-ups, call 'em crunches or ab-blasters, it doesn't matter. As with push-ups, there's a damn good reason they're a staple of any training routine. We're not chasing the mythical six-pack abs here, just a strong abdominal wall of muscle to protect your insides, help you stay upright, and provide leverage and power for your upper body. This ain't a neck exercise, buddy, so fold your arms across your chest or put them on your ears, but never behind your head. With your arms on your chest, there's zero chance of injuring your neck and it's harder to cheat. Bend your legs, with your feet firmly planted on the ground about shoulder width apart. Now squeeze and use your abdominals to lift your upper back off the ground until your shoulders have some air under them. You should be looking at the ceiling, not your knees. Then slowly lower your shoulders back to the start position. Do as many as you can. After a few dozen crunches, your neck might hurt from trying to hold that 13-pound bowling ball head of yours all by itself. If that's the case, put your hands on the *sides* of your head for a little extra support.

Crunch

Like the push-up, crunches are a workout cliché, but provide a solid payoff. Your feet should be flat on the floor, your legs at a 45-degree angle. Look up at the ceiling, not your knees during the crunch. Your hands should either be crossed on your chest or on the side of your head, never behind it. Crunch up until your shoulders are off the floor, pause briefly and then return to the start position.

Bridge

Doing a bridge looks deceptively easy, but isn't. Assume the position shown, your weight on your forearms and toes, back slightly arched. Hold for one minute or as long as you can.

Bridge: Get into a push-up position with your weight on your forearms and toes. Your body should form a straight line from head to heels. Keep your back straight, pull your abdominals in, and hold them. Hold the bridge position for one minute, or if that's too hard, do a combination of reps (repetitions) until it adds up to 60 seconds.

Side Bridge

If you've discovered how tough a front bridge really is, the side bridge will be another welcome challenge. Lying on your side as shown, weight on one forearm and one foot, hold for one minute, or as long as you can. Then do the other side.

Side Bridge: Lie on your side, with back and body straight and hold for one minute. Change sides and repeat. Yeah, this one is tough. That's why you need to start doing it.

Superman: This is the best lower back exercise you can do. Lie facedown on a mat, arms and legs straight out just like Superman. Now lift your arms and legs off the floor and hold this position for 10 seconds (count one-thousand-one, etc.). Return to the start position, then repeat until you've done a minute's time flying like Superman (six repetitions).

Reverse Crunch: Lie faceup on the floor with your arms straight above you. Roll your hips up, bringing your knees toward your chest. Straighten your legs as your lower back comes off the floor and get your toes above your head. Do 20 repetitions.

Chin-Up: Everybody fixates on building a bigger chest because they can see it in the mirror, but a strong upper

Chin-Up

The one piece of equipment every racer should have at home or easily at hand is a chin-up bar. There are few better ways to build upper body strength. Grab the bar, with arms extended but not to the point where you're hanging there. Pull yourself up (pull-ups are with your palms facing you; chin-ups are with your palms facing away from you) until your chin clears the bar, and then slowly lower yourself back to the start position. Do the exercise smoothly and you're doing it properly. Do as many as you can.

back is as important or more so. Grab the chin-up bar with an underhand, shoulder-width grip and hang with your elbows slightly bent Now pull yourself up until your chin is above the bar, hold for a second, and slowly lower your body back to the start position. Repeat until failure.

Modified Chin-Up: If it's hard to do even one chin-up from the hanging position, crouch on a chair placed under the chin-up bar to get started. Over time, you'll build enough strength to be able to do it without the chair.

PULL-UP VARIATIONS

Are regular chin-ups and pull-ups too easy for you? Try these variations:

One-Handed Pull-Up: One hand on the bar, palm facing you, while your free hand wraps around your wrist. Do as many as you can, rest, and then switch hands. Repeat.

Wide Grip Pull-Up: Palms facing away from you, spread your arms out to more than the usual shoulder width. This is a tough one.

Towel Pull-Up: Loop two towels over a bar. Grab the towels and pull yourself up. Builds a strong grip!

Pull-up: A pull-up is done with palms facing away from you, working your upper back and triceps in a different way. With your hands a little more than shoulder width apart, pull yourself slowly up, then slowly lower yourself. Don't be jerky and don't lower yourself until your arms are completely straight because it's hard on the shoulder joints. Repeat until failure.

Modified Pull-Up: If a regular, full body-weight pull-up is too difficult, you can do a modified pull-up where part of your weight is supported by your legs. It still works the upper body and over time, it will get you to where you can do a regular pull-up. Either place a chair under a high pull-up bar, or use an adjustable bar positioned low enough so you can lie underneath it with the bar a bit over an arm's length above you. Grasp the bar and pull yourself up slowly and lower yourself slowly.

Wall Sit: Your quadriceps are hardworking muscles because they help support you by straightening and stabilizing the knee joint. Quads are also what allow you to clamp the tank with your legs when riding. The stronger your quads are, the better, and this exercise will work them hard. Stand with your back against a wall, legs and knees about

Wall Sit

The wall sit is another deceptively simple and easy exercise, but it works your quads in a big way. With a wall behind you, lower yourself into a sitting position, your knees no more than a fist's width apart. Keep your arms folded and start counting "one-thousand-one." If you can get up to "one-thousand-sixty" you're in really good shape.

a fist's-width apart. Bend your knees and lower yourself into a sitting position, keeping those legs about a fist apart. Fold your arms and hold the position for one minute if you can.

Lunge: Stand with both feet together, hands by your hips. Take one long step forward so your front foot is 2 to 3 feet in front of you and lower your body until the top of your thigh is parallel to the floor. Your forward knee should be over your toes (and not extended any further). Now quickly push yourself back to the starting position. Do 10 reps for each leg. Work up to doing three sets of 10 reps per leg or add dumbbells for additional intensity [see Chapter 7]. You can modify a standard lunge with more directions and really enhance the training benefits. After returning to the start position, step to one side, return, and then step to the other side, return, and then step forward. That's one set of a multi-planar lunge.

Dips: While it requires a bench or a pair of sturdy chairs, dips are a don't-skip exercise if you want strong shoulders. I use a series of park benches that are on my running route to add dips to my endurance work out, running from bench to bench. With your feet in front of you, heels on the ground or floor, slide off the bench so your arms are supporting your upper body and your butt is hanging in the air. Slowly lower yourself until your butt is close to the ground and then return to the start position. Do the dip smoothly, no jerking. Do 10 reps and work up to doing 3 or 4 sets.

Squats: This isn't the weight-lifting version, but it's more than tough enough. If you have knee problems, you're excused from doing this one, because squats require flexibility and put some stress on knee joints. With your arms held out in front of you, inhale deeply and then slowly descend into the squat. Concentrate on sitting back and placing your body weight on your heels. Your back should not arch forward. Descend slowly until the tops of your thighs are parallel with the floor. Now drive yourself upright with power, driving your heels into the floor as your hips move up and forward. That's one set. Repeat until you have done it 100 times.

Front squats are a way to warm up and build your legs all at the same time. From an upright standing position with your arms held straight out in front of your body, lower yourself in a smooth motion until your thighs are parallel with the floor. Keep your arms stretched out in front of you and then return to the start position. Keep repeating the squat without stopping for one minute or 100 squats or some similar combination. This is a deceptively simple but very effective work out.

Front Squat

Hindu Squat: This is essentially the same, except your arms go from in front of you to down by your sides at an angle, and then are swung back up so they're in front again. It provides more work for your arms and shoulders.

Leg Raises: Lie on the floor, arms to your sides with your hands tucked under your lower back. Raise your legs together so they're no more than 6 inches off the floor and hold for one minute (it's going to be a very long, and painful

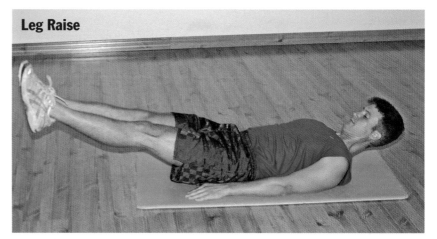

Leg Raise

Want to find out how strong your abs really are? The leg raise is your barometer. Lying on the floor, hands under the small of your back, raise your legs until they're no more than a foot off the floor. Hold for one minute, or as long as you can. If you can't do one continuous minute, do multiple sets until they add up to a minute's time.

minute), even if you have to do the minute in segments.

Big Balls

Those giant balls in bright colors you see in gyms, often being used by the spandex-clad babes, aren't just a passing fad. Exercise balls have become a standard part of many training programs. They go by various labels, but whether you call them Swiss, stability, balance, or exercise balls, the concept is the same. The ball forces your muscles to work harder. Specifically:

• Working on a curved surface forces your midsection muscles to contract constantly, even when you're targeting other muscle groups.

• The ball forces more muscles into action, because the ball is inherently unstable. Your body's stabilizer muscles, which are often ignored in training, are forced to go to work and build strength in muscles you probably didn't even know existed.

• Your abs work through their full range of motion because the shape of the ball means you start the movements in a pre-stretched position.

• The ball teaches your muscles to work together, as they have to do in real life and sports, rather than individually and in isolation as happens with strength-training machines.

• When using dumbbells and an exercise ball, lighter weight dumbbells are the rule, but the strength gains from the stabilizing muscles mean you'll be able to work with heavier weights when going back to a conventional weight bench.

• Doing exercises on the ball helps your overall balance.

You need the right size ball for your height. Here's how to pick one:

Up to 4'8"   45 cm ball
4'8" to 5'3"   55 cm
5'3" to 6'   65 cm
Over 6'   75 cm

If your height puts you right at the end of the ball size spectrum, go with the next larger size. Cheap ones will be around $15, but even the most expensive will only be around $50. Spend a little more to get better quality because you'll be using it a lot. Shop around for the best price because a lot of places sell them. If it doesn't come with a pump, as long as you have an air compressor in the garage, you don't need to buy one. But if you don't have an air compressor, then buy the pump—trust me, you'll be glad you did.

Ball Crunch

Exercise (also called Swiss or stability) balls aren't a gimmick. Because they force your muscles to work harder to keep things stabilized, the workout benefits are real because it's harder to keep the ball in place than you might think. Buy one and use them for a new approach to crunches as shown here.

Push-Up

For this push-up variation, start out with your stomach on the ball and slide–forward until your legs are the only thing keeping you in place. Do your pushups while keeping the ball in place—much tougher than it looks.

Exercise Ball Training

Here's a sample of a few of the exercises you should do with a stability ball. You'll find it amazing how much more difficult some basic exercises become once you add a stability ball to the picture. This is only a sampling of possible exercises.

Obliques

For: Abdominals, obliques
Lie sideways on the ball, with your legs straight and braced against a wall. Hold your hands behind your ears. Lift your shoulder and crunch sideways toward your hip, holding for a second before returning. Don't twist. Do a set, then switch sides.

Push-Up

For: Chest, shoulders, upper back
Start out with your stomach on the ball and then roll forward until your knees or shins are still on the ball. Do a standard push-up (it's going to be harder than you think). For a tougher work out, roll forward until only your feet are on the ball.

Prone Reverse Fly

For: Shoulders, upper back
Prone reverse flies are good for your shoulders and upper back. The stability ball limits your range of motion, which helps build those neglected back muscles. People usually focus on the chest rather than the back, but they shouldn't. Lie on your chest on the ball and lift a light set of dumbbells out, as if you're trying to fly.

Stabilizing Push-Up

For: Triceps
Place your arms 8 to 10 inches apart on a ball that's a little bit in front of you (the farther away you are, the harder the exercise becomes). With a straight back and your weight on the balls of your feet, do push-ups. Try to pull your abdominal muscles in toward your spine as you do this.

TWO-MINUTE BOARD

- Your core muscles are the ones you build your training around. Without a solid core structure as a foundation, you can't build yourself up.
- Core work outs are done as part of other work outs.
- Core work outs can be done just about anywhere so they're perfect for travel, when you're stuck at the office, or when you don't feel like going to the gym.
- Warming up and stretching. Warming up is always required, while stretching is optional.
- Jumping rope is an excellent warm-up which also improves your timing and balance.
- Stretch on a case-by-case basis depending on what works best for you.
- The big exercise balls you see in health clubs are a very useful piece of training gear. So good, you should have one at home.

Do a standard pushup with the ball in front of you. You have to both keep the ball from rolling away, and of course the pushup itself. Besides working all the usual muscles, your reflexes will get a workout.

Chapter 5

EATING TO WIN

Thanks to the typical American diet, a nasty part of our culture that we've managed to export to other countries, the average American is now more likely to be obese than not. As of 2005, a full two-thirds of the U.S. population were medically classified as obese. As a nation, we should be ashamed and profoundly embarrassed by that statistic. Instead, we've gotten so used to people being fat that many people now consider being overweight the norm, not the exception. That's about the saddest thing I can think of saying.

Since four of the top ten causes of death in the United States are directly linked to our bad diet choices, you can see just how serious our nation's addiction to food has become. It's not about how we look, it's about our national health.

Modern life, however, makes what used to be a simple task incredibly difficult. It's why so many people are fat and why obesity is now a global health threat. More people are going to die this year from obesity-related illnesses than from fatal diseases like AIDS. In many cases, it could've been avoided.

Good intentions about eating right simply aren't enough. Food is marketed to us nonstop, hard and relentlessly. Billions of dollars are spent on ads numbering in the thousands that encourage us to eat more and more. Visiting a restaurant or fast food franchise is treated as a requirement for a happy life, rather than a personal choice. Little kids believe that a meal consists of fried high-calorie food packaged with a cheap toy for their tubby little mitts. School cafeterias serve junk food and have pop machines installed for the profits they bring in, reinforcing bad diet choices rather than promoting

Want to fly high? The less extra weight your body is carrying, the faster (and higher) you'll go.

Want to lose weight and keep it off? It's simple to do. Just avoid the drive-thru lines and *never* visit any of the fast food joints. Make your own healthy lunch and pack it to work or school. You'll spend less, eat better, and the pounds will melt off if you're also working out. Banning fast food from your diet is the single best diet change you can make.

It's a war for our health and it's a battle we're losing. We spend billions buying too much food with too little nutritional value, then turn around and spend billions more on diet plans, diet foods (an oxymoron), diet books, and health club memberships. It's the new circle of life.

Flab is Your Enemy

For a racer, excess flab is the enemy. You wouldn't choose to bolt 20 pounds of chrome gee-gaws to your handlebars, slowing it down and making it more difficult to control, yet many riders knowingly carry a sizable spare tire of fat around their middles. These are usually the same dudes who obsess over getting their race bikes as lightweight as possible.

sound nutrition. This is taking place as school sports and physical education classes are being eliminated due to budget cuts. Kids are being set up for the same lifetime health problems as their overweight, short-of-breath, cholesterol-drug-taking, diabetic parents.

All the food company marketing muscle is geared toward making us eat too much of the wrong stuff. Restaurant portions are out of control and filled with enough calories to satisfy a pair of hungry NFL linebackers. Grocery aisles are lined with heavily advertised, high-sugar/salt/fat foods that have the cunning combination of being horrible for us physically and much too delicious to ignore.

Whether it's on your body or on the bike, flab slows you down. Being fat also opens you up to a host of health problems that can substantially shorten your life, limit what you can do in your spare time, and even put an end to your riding altogether. Yes, I know some of you reading this are captives in a big-boned, genetically determined double XL-sized body. Even if Mother Nature gave you an XXL-size body, you can still lose some of that weight and replace it with muscle by putting forth some effort.

Always remember that your bike hates fat! Extra pounds mean it has to work that much harder to haul your lard ass around. All the carbon fiber and titanium go-fast goodies in the world will only melt a few pounds off the bike, but weight is weight, whether you're wearing it or riding it. Making a modern race bike 10 pounds lighter costs thousands of dollars, but losing the same amount from your body is very doable and a whole lot less expensive.

Food, diets, eating habits, weight loss, healthy cooking, and related topics can easily fill an entire book. It's a big, complex, and confusing topic with as much pop psychology involved as nutrition. We're not going to go there. Instead, what follows are simple ways to get your diet into shape and keep it there while you're also getting yourself into racing shape.

CALCULATE YOUR BODY MASS INDEX (BMI)

The Body Mass Index (BMI) is a somewhat crude calculation of whether you're overweight or not. Based on height and weight, it doesn't take into account how much of your body weight is muscle, so you can actually be very fit and strong and be considered overweight according to the BMI tables. However, I think you know whether or not you're sleek and strong or pudgy and weak. You can go online to numerous websites and plug in the numbers to get your BMI, but all you really need is a calculator. Here's the formula for someone who's 6 feet tall and weighs 165 lbs:

Multiply your height in inches (e.g.: 72 inches) by itself (72 x 72 = 5,184)
Divide your weight by that number (165/5184 = .0318)
Multiply that number by 704.5 (.0318 x 704.5 = 22.4 BMI)

If your number is between 18.5 and 24.9 you're at low risk of major diseases and at an optimal weight. Under those numbers and you're too light; over them and you're overweight.

PORTION SIZE

W e've gotten so used to supersized meals that we no longer recognize normal, healthy portion sizes. Here's what a normal portion should actually look like:

3 oz of meat (recommended size per meal)	deck of cards or a bar of soap
3 oz of fish	size of a checkbook
8 oz of meat	size of a thin paperback book
1 oz of cheese	your index finger or 4 dice
1 cup of cooked pasta	size of a tennis ball
Bagel (normal sized)	size of a hockey puck
1 cup of cereal or 1 medium baked potato	size of your fist

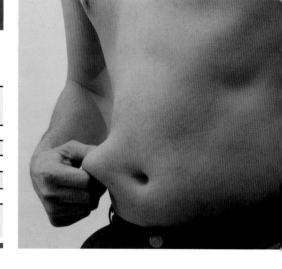

Diet is a Noun, Not a Verb

Every independent study of weight-loss diets has reached the same conclusion: None of them work more than temporarily, if at all. Every fad diet, including all the heavily advertised ones with their own books and grocery store foods, is so much wishful thinking. It's not that following these diets means you won't lose some weight, but the odds are very much against keeping it off.

Diets don't work. If you want to lose weight and stay in control of your waistline, you need to use your brain. Yeah, that thing between your ears is the best tool you have for weight control. I want you to learn how to make good, intelligent decisions about food and your eating habits. You need to approach eating with the same discipline you apply to the rest of your training.

Weight loss and weight control involve simple mathematics. The 2+2 kind of math you learned in first grade: You lose weight when you burn more calories than you consume. Burning those calories means doing something active every day, while intelligently— that brain thing again—choosing the types and quantities of food you eat.

I don't believe in dieting and you shouldn't either. In fact, you have my permission to eat whatever you want. All I suggest, whether you're overweight now or not, is to actually think about what you're eating. Don't just mindlessly shove stuff into your mouth. You don't have to

eliminate any foods or put yourself on some type of bread-and-water starvation regime as long as you think about your diet choices first. Your brain is the best weight-control tool you have.

"Diet" should be a noun when you hear it, meaning you consciously choose what you eat, how it's prepared, and understand the calorie consequences of *your* choices. Forget about fad diets ("diet" as a verb) and focus on eating properly and balancing what you eat with the amount of exercise you're doing. It's really no more complex than that.

Weight Loss for Racers

If you're already carrying more than 10 pounds of excess blubber to the start line, you should combine the work outs in this book with the additional goal of getting your weight under control. The sooner you lose that extra poundage, the sooner you'll be able to train harder, better, and more efficiently.

Not sure if you're overweight? Check the chart on page 53 for healthy weights based on the Body Mass Index (BMI). While the BMI has some statistical flaws, it's still a pretty accurate guide to whether or not your weight is within healthy norms.

Just as following a training plan requires discipline, dedication, and a no-blink focus on your goals, weight loss requires the same no-compromise attitude. Fortunately, it's pretty easy to

Diets won't fix your weight problem. Instead, change your whole approach to food. Know what you're eating and the caloric hit you pay. It's simple math that anybody can understand.

remember what you need to do and within a week or two, the steps involved will be second nature—or they should be.

Getting your weight under control involves five simple adjustments on your part:

1. Eat sensibly and eat the right types of foods. That means three daily meals that are heavy on fruit and vegetables and light on fats, sugar, and alcohol.

2. Exercise daily, both cardio and muscle-building exercises. Strength training helps you lose more fat and tones your muscles, so you look better as well.

3. Reshape your eating behaviors, especially the ones that lead to overeating. Know how many calories you need each day and stay on target. Yes, there are ways to get past the daily snack attacks.

4. Keep a food diary, especially at the beginning of any weight loss attempt. Guys tend to underestimate the number of calories they're eating and overestimate how much exercise they're getting. A food diary will be an eye-opener for most people. The food diary, combined with your work out log, will help you adjust your meals and keep you honest and motivated.

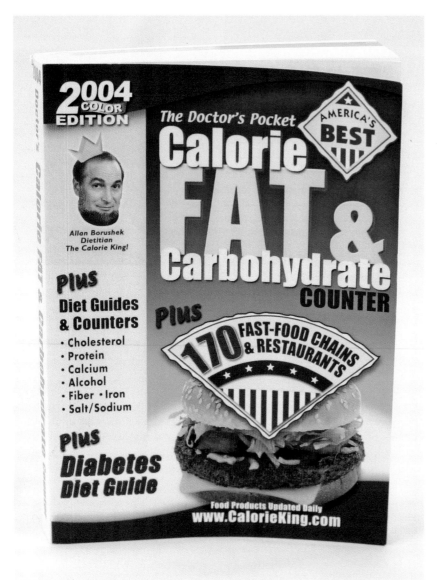

This pocket-size book has the calorie, fat, and carbohydrate totals for just about every food and restaurant meal you are likely to encounter. To take charge of your eating habits, find out how many calories you really require—probably around 2,000 calories a day—and then use this book to see how many you're actually consuming each day. That's step one.

5. Get some moral support. Telling friends, family, racing buddies, and co-workers that you're going to weigh a specific weight by a specific time is a great motivator because your friends help keep you focused on your goal. Print your goals out and tape the pages up around your office, your garage, and in your car as reminders. Especially when the reminders are in your vehicle, it's a great deterrent to hitting the drive-thru window for a double gut-buster deluxe.

Winning The Food War

The above tactics are the rough framework for how you lose weight, but you also need some specific weight loss techniques. While the calories-in/calories-burned math is pretty simple, modern society is so geared to encouraging overeating, that you need to learn how to fight back. Call the following advice "Defensive Eating Tips." Think of them as ways to defend your body from gaining weight in a culture that saturates us in "eat more" messages.

Use these methods to gain control of your eating habits and lose weight:

• Eat breakfast every single day. Your mom probably told you a million times that breakfast is the most important meal of the day, and surprise, she's absolutely right (Call her up right now and tell her thank you). You should eat your largest meal in the morning, which is when your body has gone the longest without food. A good, healthy breakfast fuels your body for the day ahead and helps prevent overeating at lunch and dinner. When you skip breakfast, you're training your body to store fat to get you through the morning hours.

• Eat the most at breakfast, the least at dinner. This is the opposite of how people approach meals in our culture, but we're no longer an agrarian society where giant evening meals are necessary to refuel us from the hard physical labor we endured during the day. Now most of us work at sedentary jobs or sit in school, drive everywhere, and have few chances to burn up calories. Our dining habits need to change accordingly.

• Know how many calories you really need and keep an eye on the daily total. See the sidebar for online resources to help you calculate this amount.

• Eat fruit and veggies, not chip and dip (What? You thought I was going to endorse your love of fried pork rinds?). If you make no other changes to your lifestyle, this is the biggie.

• Train your family to eat as they should. You do this by taking charge of the grocery shopping.

• A "portion" is never larger than your fist and usually is much smaller.

• Be flexible, be disciplined, but be realistic. Few people can follow rigid dietary restrictions for long, so give yourself permission to splurge now and then as a reward for being good the rest of the time.

The trenches of the war for control of your waistline are the grocery store aisles. Take charge of the grocery shopping so you can keep the junk in your cupboards and refrigerator to a minimum.

• Cook it yourself. It's cheaper, easier (really), and all-around better for you. If you don't know how to cook, learn. If you can do a top-end rebuild, you can learn which knobs to turn on the stove.

• Food is fuel. Always think about how much fuel you really need to get through that day's activities. You wouldn't fill up your bike to where's it's overflowing and gas is pouring onto the ground, so why would you do that with your body?

• Learn the food marketing tricks and how to ignore them. Read the labels, dude! See the sidebar for details.

• "Diet" is a noun and should refer to what you choose to eat. Diet as a verb should not refer to what you're constantly doing. Diets don't work.

• Put yourself in charge of the grocery shopping. Stop buying junk food, candy, any type of pop that isn't diet, foods that require frying, sausage, cookies, donuts, hot dogs, and fatty meats. Fill the grocery cart with fruits, vegetables (French fries don't count, sorry), whole grain cereals, oatmeal, lean cuts of meat, turkey, and skinless chicken breasts. By putting yourself in charge of the grocery buying, you also train your family to eat healthier, which makes it easier for *you* to eat better—sneaky but necessary. It's not enough to make a list and let somebody else shop because they'll just buy the same crappy junk and sooner or later (mostly sooner), you'll find yourself chowing down on a fat-drenched, calorie-filled Cup O' Lard goodie.

• You can tell how you're doing in terms of healthy eating by looking at the grocery cart before checkout. If you see nothing but packaged convenience foods, bags of chips, frozen ready-to-eat meals, and chocolate desserts, you're in trouble. Your shopping cart should have a top layer of fresh fruits and vegetables, whole grain bread and cereals, eggs, lean cuts of meat (preferably fish, chicken, or turkey), and nothing to drink that lists "sugar" or "corn syrup" as the first ingredient.

• Downsize your plates. Big plates invite big servings which lead to big butts.

• Avoid buffet-style restaurants and any fast food franchise, period. Doing this is in the no-brainer category. I'll make an exception for Subway because many of their sandwiches are good

HOW TO READ A FOOD LABEL

You need to learn the basics of reading a product's food label if you want to control your weight. While the labels are required by law and carry a lot of information, they can still be misleading. The number of "servings" per package hardly ever matches what you'd actually consume.

The labels on food packages are there by law, and for good reason. If you can understand the information (it's getting easier with each revision), it allows you to make more intelligent eating decisions. Here's the Cliff Notes version of the key information you need to check:

Serving Size: This is the basis for all the numbers that follow. A "serving" is supposed to be the amount people should or would consume of the food. That's okay, but food marketers are putting multiple servings into one box, bottle, or bag. Then the label makes it seem the actual calorie hit is smaller than it really is. *Calories:* The number per serving. Let's say the label says 100 calories, but the servings per container are four; that means if you finish off the whole bottle, you just chugged 400 calories.

Calories from Fat: Again, it's per serving, so do the math.

Trans Fat: Avoid any items high in trans fat. Zero is the number you want to see here. Trans fat is now the acknowledged villain in heart disease and other illnesses.

Total Carbohydrates: This includes all kinds of carbs, simple and complex. You want little of the simple carbs and lots of the complex, but so far, there's no way to tell what the ratio is just by reading the label.

Dietary Fiber: Fiber is good for you and has no calories. You don't get enough, so go looking for more.

Ingredients: Listed by largest amount to the smallest. This means a food contains the largest amount of the first item listed and the smallest of the last item on the list. Be especially on the lookout for "high fructose corn syrup" which sounds almost healthy, but causes weight gain. It's a sugar substitute that food companies use because it's much cheaper than sugar. Studies have shown it promotes quicker weight gain that's also harder to lose.

---

meals without being burdened with globs of added fat. Yes, Jared really did lose all that weight by only eating at Subway—it's a true story.

• Drink a lot of water. Take a water bottle to work, keep it on your desk, and refill as needed. Thirst is often confused as hunger, so stay hydrated all day long.

• Little things add up. If you add cream and sugar to your coffee, that's a lot of calories you could easily do without. This is where a food diary can be very revealing because it shows where the little things in your diet have big repercussions. Learn to drink your coffee black or switch to no-cal substitutes.

• Beware of all the calorie-loaded landmines out there. The donuts in the meeting room, the latte deluxe at the coffee shop, the Girl Scout cookie sales pitch, and the candy or pizza rewards for working late or getting a good grade.

• Beware also of the healthy-sounding foods that have "light" or "nonfat" labels. While these are usually better for you than consuming the full-fat versions, they still have calories, sometimes quite a lot of them, and those calories still count against your daily total.

• Learn how to read and understand food labels [see the sidebar]. Note the portion size and the calorie count per serving. Often the serving size listed is ridiculous and has nothing to do with how much someone would actually consume. Ever known anyone to eat only one-third of a bag of chips? Me neither. It's a game that food marketers play to convince you something is less fattening than it really is.

• Pack your own lunch rather than going out with the gang at noon. Better yet, take a walk to someplace pleasant and have your lunch outside. Pack sandwiches made with lean turkey or chicken, nonfat mayo, mustard, some spinach leaves, tomato, and onion to get some vegetables into your diet. Besides saving money that you can spend on new go-faster bike goodies, you'll be eating better and have more time to take a calorie-burning walk or spend some time at the gym.

• Do your work out at lunch time. I've done this for a couple of decades, using lunch time as my best chance for a run, followed by a quick, light lunch. While everyone else is piling on calories, I'm burning them up. If your job allows you to do your training at lunch time, do it. It's the ideal time of the day to get some exercise and recharge your internal batteries so you're ready for the rest of the day. It also leaves your evenings free for other things or another work out, sports league or working on the race bike.

BACK FROM THE BAN

Over the years, certain foods got banned from our diets because they were suspected as being bad for our health. Well, later studies proved that some banned foods aren't dietary bad boys after all, so you can put them back into your diet if you so choose.

Cheese: Yes, many cheeses are high fat, but they're also good sources of calcium and contain linoleic acid, a "good" fat that fights disease and (strange as it may sound) fat storage in your body.

Dark Chocolate: It contains some of the same disease-fighting antioxidants found in fruits and vegetables, and the main fat in dark chocolate doesn't raise cholesterol. Chocolate is a mood booster because it increases serotonin in the brain. Milk chocolate is what you want to avoid.

Beef: Beef is an excellent source of protein and such nutrients as iron, zinc, and vitamin B12. Just choose the lean cuts, skipping the prime rib and T-bones, which have twice as much fat and calories as leaner cuts.

Eggs: Eggs got chased off our menus because they're high in cholesterol, but researchers now know that saturated fat is the real enemy in heart disease. Eggs are low in fat, a good source of protein, and contain important nutrients. Skip the fatty sausage side dishes.

Nuts: Yes, they're high in fat, but it's the good monounsaturated fat, which reduces your risk of heart disease. Besides packing a potent nutrient load, nuts make you feel full faster, so they are a good snack, in moderation.

• Try different and healthier foods cooked in the least fattening way, generally grilled or baked. One more reason to put yourself in charge of groceries. Over time, your body and taste buds adjust to less fatty, less salty, healthier foods. Initially, you may have to teach yourself to like skim milk, yogurt (an excellent nutrient source), diet soda, sugar substitutes such as Splenda, and other low-cal foods, but over time they become what you prefer and fatty foods become unpalatable. Remember that you're in a war here, a battle to reclaim your body and maintain your good health. You can never let down your guard.

• Got the munchies attack at work or school? Instead of heading for the vending machines and their rows of sugar- and fat-soaked joys, have a personal stash of nuts, dried fruit, peanuts, and raisins in a desk drawer. Dried fruit especially provides a slow, steady energy boost, compared to the short-lived jolt from a candy bar.

Eat breakfast and make it a healthy one. It fuels you up for the whole day, helps keep you from overeating at lunch, and makes it easier to ignore the box of donuts somebody brought to the staff meeting. Breakfast is the most important meal of the day, just like your mom told you.

- Protein keeps your appetite in check longer than sugar or fat. A turkey or tuna sandwich will do more to keep you feeling full than a sugary snack.

- Eat more fish, more fruits, more vegetables, and more whole-grain cereal products. All are important parts of your diet, you don't get enough of them, they fill you up while providing essential nutrients, and all are underrepresented in the typical American diet. The short version: They do a better job of filling you up without filling you out.

- Unless you've gone 12 hours without any food whatsoever, avoid fast food franchises. Even though they've started to offer healthier fare, you're likely to drop into old, bad habits and order the double gut-buster with bacon and cheese.

ETHNIC DINING

You can probably figure out how healthy your normal meals are or aren't, but when dining out at ethnic restaurants, it can be uncharted waters. Here's a map:

Asian: Since most dishes emphasize veggies and only small amounts of meat, many menu choices are good as long as they're not breaded, swimming in oil, or tempura. Best choices are stir fry dishes, and steamed brown rice rather than fried.

Mexican: This cuisine boasts lots of deep-fried bad choices, many with layers of cheese as an artery-clogging bonus. Best options are grilled chicken or fish dishes, especially fajitas or carnitas.

Italian: As with Mexican, there are lots of cheesy dishes and creamy sauces. Keep it simple and go with basic red sauces, chicken and fish instead of sausage, and beware of the calorie load from the garlic bread.

French: Go with grilled fish and chicken and hold the sauces, especially the creamy ones like béarnaise, béchamel, and hollandaise. Croissants have about 12 times the fat as plain ol' French bread.

Cajun: Hush puppies are deep-fried dough, and you know what that means. Also avoid anything made with roux, a mixture of flour and fat. Skip the dirty rice, but order blackened seafood and chicken dishes.

Yes, it's possible to keep your weight under control even during the holidays or on vacation. Instead of surrendering to what you consider inevitable, use the holiday free time to ramp up your exercise hours. Most large cities have Thanksgiving Day runs. The point is you can find ways to work out and keep the caloric tidal wave from overwhelming you.

program require adequate sleep so your muscles can recover and build up stronger, but recent scientific studies show that people who don't sleep enough end up gaining weight. It's apparently one way the body responds to being cheated on the sleep it needs.

• Forget about three squares a day and graze instead. Eating small amounts five or six times a day works well for some people. Grazing, as it's called, actually matches the way our remote ancestors lived and ate.

• Salads aren't the answer. Lettuce itself is not especially nutritious—it's the wimp of the veggie world—and most salad dressings are flavored liquid fat. Especially bad are the salads being sold by the fast-food chains as a healthy alternative. They're usually loaded with additions that raise the fat content to the level of a burger. If you like salads, make your own using fresh spinach and low-fat or vinegar-based dressing.

• Watch portion sizes. In restaurants, especially, super-sized portions are now the rule and we're being trained to expect a giant portion as the norm. It's not. You don't need that much food—nobody does. One of the true pleasures in life is dining out and you don't have to give that up, but you need to know when to put your fork down and say "no more." Sharing your entrée is one way of dealing with the super-sizing dilemma or take the extra food home. They're making you pay for two meals' worth of calories, so treat it that way by taking the extra home for later.

Start a Food Diary

We're guys. Guys always eat and drink more than they think they do and they always overestimate how much exercise they're getting. Always. It's a natural law.

It's guaranteed that you're eating more than you think you are. Even when you think you're being careful and have cut down on the junk food, you'd be surprised to see how many calories you're really consuming. Modern life presents us with lots of hidden caloric

Some foods that were once classified as bad for your health have now been reconsidered. Eggs are one of them, eaten in moderation.

• On road trips (something racers do a lot of), take along a bag or cooler full of healthy snacks, a turkey sandwich, water or diet soda, and other good things. Besides saving money by not having to purchase a gas station's overpriced junk food, you'll be less likely to take that exit with all the fast-food signs beckoning.

• Splurge occasionally. You're human, so accept the fact that you're not going to be a health saint and always eat only the right stuff. Do it knowingly, without agonizing over it, and then return to your healthy eating habits with the next meal.

• Get enough sleep. Really. Not only do the demands of your training

This is either a sign that you need to lose some weight or to check your suspension settings.

landmines and calories pile up like football players chasing a fumble.

You know that to keep your weight under control, you have to burn as many calories as you consume. If you are already overweight, you need to lower your caloric intake. To lose one pound of fat, you have to create a 3,500 calorie deficit. That's the simple math of it all. To both lose weight and train yourself to develop healthy eating habits, start a food diary.

A food diary can be as simple as a notebook, a portion of your daily calendar planner, preprinted diaries from the bookstore or computerized versions which do the math for you. Using a food diary is simple: Just note what you ate, how many calories it had, and the calories burned off that day from exercise and work. At the end of the day, add it all up so that you'll have a clear picture of what you're doing right and wrong. You can also base your future meals on your calorie target for the day.

How do you figure out the calories? A trip to your nearest bookstore should get you a copy of *The Doctor's Pocket Calorie Fat & Carbohydrate Counter*. It's about $7 and contains the calorie totals of just about every commonly available food in the USA. Fast foods, veggies, snacks, restaurant meals . . . just about everything you can buy and eat, healthy or not. The book's information is regularly updated online, to keep it current. The small size of this book allows you to carry it along for easy reference. You'll also find quite a bit of good advice about eating healthier, without a lot of preaching—just straightforward common sense. For more information, visit www.calorieking.com.

Besides tracking calories, you should take a long, hard look at where those calories are coming from. Americans eat too much fat. It's easy to do because fat tastes good. Ideally, for both your health and weight control, your daily intake shouldn't have more than 30% of the calories coming from fat. For an average-size adult male, that's 25 grams of fat per day. To put that in perspective, a Quarter Pounder with

cheese has 30 grams of fat. something to think about the next time you have the fast-food burger urge.

You can choose to keep a food diary forever . . . or only for a week or two. Use it the way that works best for you to keep tabs on what you're eating. Since this is the start of your training program, keep one for at least the first few weeks of your training so you can see where the calories are coming from. The numbers will probably scare you, which makes it a great starting point for learning to eat better.

How Many Calories Do I Need?

There's no simple answer to the question of how many daily calories you need, because there are so many variables involved. Your activity level, height, sex, age, metabolism, body type, and whether you're trying to lose weight or gain it are just some of the factors.

For example, the average-size adult male who sits behind a desk most of the day and little else, needs only about 1,800 to 2,200 calories. The same guy with a physically active job or heavy work out schedule will need 2,600 to 2,800 calories. Take it up to the elite training level, and that same man riding in the Tour de France, battling up mountain passes and pedaling over 100 miles daily, will need 9,000 calories daily to keep his muscles fueled.

Since you're riding a dirt bike, an active sport, your calorie needs are going to be a bit higher than the lard butt who never does anything except channel surf. But unless you're riding several times a week while also following a good work out plan, you still probably only need about 2,000 to 2,500 calories a day. Adjust that number to a couple hundred less if you're trying to slim down. Even on days when

HEALTHY WEIGHTS

This chart is based on body weights within the preferred, healthy Body Mass Index (BMI) of 20 to 25. Note that the BMI is not very accurate if you're a heavily muscled and very active athlete.

Height (no shoes)	Healthy Weight Range
4'9"	92-114 lbs
4'10"	97-121 lbs
4'11"	99-123 lbs
5'	101-127 lbs
5'1"	105-132 lbs
5'2"	110-136 lbs
5'3"	112-140 lbs
5'5"	119-149 lbs
5'6"	123-156 lbs
5'7"	127-158 lbs
5'8"	129-162 lbs
5'9"	134-167 lbs
5'10"	138-173 lbs
5'11"	143-178 lbs
6'	145-182 lbs
6'1"	149-187 lbs
6'2"	156-193 lbs
6'3"	158-198 lbs
6'4"	162-202 lbs
6'5"	170-211 lbs

you ride for hours or work out like a mad man, you shouldn't take it to mean you've got permission to pig out afterward. Not if you want to keep your weight under control.

To run the numbers for yourself, go online and visit www.fitwatch.com. Click on the Basal Metabolic Rate (BMR) chart and input your info. You'll get your BMR expressed in calories necessary per day, giving you a starting point for estimating your daily calorie requirements.

Carb Confusion

Yes, you need carbohydrates (carbs) in your diet. Do not buy into the no-carb diet flim-flam.

Carbs, however, come in two different varieties: Simple carbs are broken down quickly in the body and rapidly raise blood sugar levels. These are called High Glycemic (GI) foods and include candy, white rice, white bread, and highly refined, sugary cereals. You'd think that a quick energy boost would be the result and to some extent this is true, but the energy spike is short-lived. Your body quickly crashes from this quick spike causing you to be tired and hungry again.

Better choices are complex carbohydrates, referred to as foods having a Low GI. Foods with a Low GI are digested and absorbed more slowly, satisfying hunger and maintaining your energy levels for much longer periods of time. Whole-grain breads, pasta, beans, fruits, and vegetables all offer Low GI complex carbs. For obvious reasons, these should be your diet choices.

The Low GI (Glycemic Index) and High GI measure is one of those pieces of information soon to be added to food labels, so you need to understand what it refers to. Summarized: Go Low.

Ten Can't-Miss Foods

These are the food types that you can't go wrong by choosing. If they're not in your diet, add them.

1. Whole-grain cereals and bread: In cereals, choose the low-fat, low-sugar, high-fiber stuff for quality carbs,

Eating to win is simple. Your meals should be based on fresh fruit, veggies, whole-grain cereals and bread, and lean cuts of meat. And zero fast food. That's "zero" as in none.

Defeat the late-afternoon munchie attack by stocking your desk drawer or locker with some quality carbs (fruit), energy bars, or a whole-grain bagel. These are the same foods you'll turn to on race day to provide long-lasting energy.

WORKING OFF THOSE NACHOS

Everything you do burns some calories, even flipping the pages of this book. Here's the approximate calorie-burn **per hour** for a 170-pound male.

Chopping wood	400 calories
Ditch digging	700 calories
Mowing the lawn (pushing a mower, not riding it)	500 calories
Painting a room	375 calories
Washing the truck	270 calories
Sex	240 calories
Cross-country skiing	660 calories
Tennis	520 calories
Walking (briskly)	430 calories
Running (per mile)	100 to 150 calories
Bicycling @ 15mph	600 calories
In-line skating	550 calories
Volleyball	400 calories

vitamins, and minerals. Pile on berries and bananas for even more good nutrition. Besides being one of the best choices for a good breakfast, use whole-grain cereals as snacks or take-along road food. Whole-grain bread and bagels are what your sandwiches require—nothing else will do.

2. Bananas: High in carbs, fiber, and potassium, bananas are prepackaged by Mom Nature and ready to eat. It doesn't get any simpler or better for you than this.

3. Low-Fat Yogurt: Protein, calcium, and active yogurt cultures promote good health. Your gut needs this stuff and dairy foods appear to help with weight loss.

4. Oranges: Vitamin C and fiber in a convenient package are a great benefit.

5. Potatoes: This vegetable is a high-energy food with tons of carbs,

Hamburgers have their place in your diet (of course!) but make them better for you. Instead of cheese, mayo, and bacon, dress it with lettuce, onion, tomato, and on a whole-grain bun. You'll be adding fiber and veggies to your meal, while sidestepping a lot of the fat.

potassium (more than a banana), and vitamins. Don't spoil it by burying it under heaps of high-fat condiments—try salsa as a topping instead.

6. Apples: Prepackaged, easy to carry, and easy to have on hand. Apples provide fiber, complex carbs, and a smorgasbord of nutrients your body needs. That old cliché about an apple a day has a lot of truth to it.

7. Pasta: Everybody likes pasta. Choose the whole-wheat versions. Pasta contributes valuable carbohydrates to match your active lifestyle. Cover with red sauces and skip the cheese.

8. Broccoli: It's the ultimate green vegetable with lots of everything, including cancer-fighting elements.

9. Tuna: An exceptional source of protein (6 ounces contains about 40 grams of protein). Mix it up with low-fat mayo, or just eat it out of the can.

10. Chicken and turkey: Meats that are essentially fat-free if you don't eat the skin; they also provide lots of muscle-building protein.

Surviving Vacation and the Holidays

Gaining weight on vacation or during the holidays is so expected that lots of people don't even bother to put up a fight. Of course, once you gain some excess poundage, you then have to find a way to get rid of it. This is why health clubs are so busy during January.

It seems like a lot of wasted effort to me. It's far simpler to never gain the extra weight in the first place than it is to take it off time after time. Since vacations and holidays are problems for everyone, here are some coping strategies:

• Take along your work out gear and start or finish each day with a run or some other form of calorie-burning exercise. A vacation means spare hours, so use some of them for yourself to maintain your fitness.

• Most large cities have Thanksgiving Day running races, so start your turkey day festivities by doing the run.

• In restaurants, watch portion sizes. Split entrees.

• Watch the alcohol use—it's mostly calories.

ONLINE HELP

Since this is the Internet Age, I won't bore you with the math behind the various formulas for things likes BMR (Basal Metabolic Rate), BMI (Body Mass Index), and so on. Let the infernal computers do the work. Surf over to the following sites for additional information and those handy electronic calculators to get a read on your personal fitness level.

www.calorie-count.com

www.calorieking.com

www.fitwatch.com

www.preventdisease.com (great site; needs a better name)

www.runnersworld.com

• Get a condo unit or extended-stay motel room that has a kitchenette. Stock the fridge with water, healthy juices, diet drinks, fruit, veggies, and other appetite suppressors.

• Don't make dining out or bar-hopping the main way to entertain.

• Carry a small cooler in the car and stock it with diet drinks, water, sandwiches, and healthy snacks as a way to completely avoid the fast food joints.

• Park farther away from attractions so you have to walk more.

• Schedule some fun physical activities that your whole family can share. Do a group bicycle ride, play volleyball, hike, swim, surf, or take a nature walk.

• Understand the lingo in restaurant menus. Words like "fried, buttery, crispy, tempura, au gratin, etouffe, sautéed, rich, creamy, and breaded" all actually spell F-A-T.

• Appetizers are almost always the fattiest and least healthy items on the menu. That's why we like them so much . . . and why we need to avoid them.

• Take your time (good advice whenever you're eating). Eat slowly rather than trying to set a record for stuffing your face.

• If you do splurge on a couple of gut-busters, don't agonize about it. We're all human. Just try to adjust your eating or your work out the next day to account for the extra calories.

TWO-MINUTE BOARD

• The typical American diet is a health- and fitness-destroying disaster.

• Diet is a noun, not a verb. Dieting doesn't work.

• Good intentions about eating right aren't enough. What you need is a new way of looking at food.

• Maintaining a healthy weight is simple math: Know how many calories you need each day and don't eat more than that amount.

• Eat breakfast every day.

• Take charge of the grocery shopping.

• One simple thing you can do that guarantees you'll lose weight: Stop going to fast food joints.

Chapter 6

ENDURANCE TRAINING

You don't usually think of it this way, but the most important muscle in your body is your heart. If it's weak, you're going to be weak. It's that simple. Fortunately, because the heart is a muscle, it can be trained to become bigger, stronger, and with more endurance.

Endurance (also called cardiovascular or aerobic) exercise is another way of saying "heart and lung training." You're stressing your heart and lungs to work harder so that over time, they'll become more efficient. It's really not any different than doing dumbbell curls to build up your biceps.

Endurance training provides a powerful base fitness level that underlies everything else you do in your training. The more efficient your body becomes at moving oxygen-rich blood to your muscles, the longer you can ride. A strong heart leads to strong legs that keep you up on the pegs longer and lets you train even harder so you can become even stronger.

You MUST do endurance training. There aren't any shortcuts here. Besides being the best way to make your heart and lungs more efficient, nothing else burns off calories and keeps your weight in control like endurance training. Aerobic training makes you tougher, both physically and mentally. Your recovery time after training sessions and between motos will be much quicker. A solid cardio program is the foundation you build the rest of your training on.

If you want to race motocross at a higher level with less fatigue and more last-lap strength, you need a solid endurance foundation. Just lifting weights or eating right isn't going to do

the job. You can have immense upper-body muscle strength, but if your lungs can't move air in and out quickly enough, you'll be as weak as a kitten about two laps into your moto. Your body can only go as fast as it can process oxygen to keep those muscles pumping away. Aerobic exercise is as necessary to a racer's training program as a bike with two wheels—you're not going anyplace without it.

Wimping Out
Cardio training is what separates the men from the boys. It's tough, rugged, requires a lot of time, and if you're doing your training outside as you should, you don't get to hang out with all the spandex-clad babes at the gym.

Because it's tough, there's at least one segment of the fitness business that says you can get the same benefits and results from strength training alone. It sounds good, but like most sounds-too-good-to-be-true claims, it's not supported by independent research. Racers need both cardiovascular and strength training, not just one or the other.

It's hard to cheat on endurance exercise. With strength training, you can choose to do 6 reps instead of 10, then decide you've done enough and hit the showers. With cardio work outs, when you're a few miles down the road from your house, if you decide to wimp out, you still have to get all the way back. Endurance work outs require commitment.

Unlike other sports, in motocross there are no timeouts, no pace laps, no teammates, no pit stops. You go as hard as you can from the time the gate drops until the checkers fly. To be as fast your last lap as on your first requires cardiovascular endurance.

The Perfect Exercise: Running

For motocross and off-road riders, running is the one form of exercise that shouldn't be skipped. It doesn't get much simpler—or much better for you—than putting down one foot after another for miles at a time. Humans were born to run. It's how evolution has shaped us.

If there's a physical reason why you absolutely cannot run, then you need to find an alternate aerobic activity. As a general guide, one mile of running is the same as three miles of cycling, eight minutes of swimming, and one mile of cross-country skiing.

Because running comes naturally for me, it took me a while to understand that many people loathe running and will do anything to avoid it. Here's an activity that comes with a couple dozen physical benefits, costs nothing in membership dues, requires very little equipment, can be done anywhere, and does more for you physically than just about any other kind of work out . . . and people want to *avoid* it? Weird logic. Running is how I train, what I do for fun, and my stress outlet when I need some time away from the suffocating press of reality.

Why Run?

Running at a mild, 10-minute/mile pace will burn more than 600 calories an hour while making your heart, lungs, and legs significantly stronger. That's a lot of calorie burn. The only other aerobic exercises that come close to offering a similar physical payback are bicycling at a solid 15-mile-per-hour pace and cross-country skiing, but both of those sports have inherent limitations of equipment, cost, geography, portability, weather, seasonal availability, and physical results. Since I believe and preach that the goal is to be healthy and fit year-round, for our whole lives, then running is a perfect match.

Running is the preferred aerobic training exercise because it's the most fundamental and simplest. The cost to play is the least (by far) and it's the one endurance sport that can be pursued

Because it's tough, people go looking for excuses to duck their endurance work outs. The weather is too hot, too cold, too wet, too windy, or even too nice to waste on a work out; it's too sunny or too dark; it's too early or it's too late; there's not enough time to do the long run you wanted to do (so you do none at all); there's a can't-miss program on TV; your knees hurt, or maybe it's the legs; you're jet-lagged or need to pack; you've got a headache or the sniffles; you're waiting for a phone call; there are a million chores and errands to do; and on and on and on.

If people put as much energy into their cardio work outs as they do in searching for excuses, they'd have their training done every day.

That should be your approach: no excuses. Go out, do what needs doing, suck it up like a man, and get it over with. You're then free to attend to all the million and one things that are so urgent. You want to be tough and fit for motocross? Then forget about making excuses.

ADDING INTENSITY

Since we know that cardio improvements require both distance PLUS intensity, here are some ways to make your runs more intense. They're a change of pace from just pounding out a few more miles, or as a way to quickly build some new endurance or a way to get a solid work out in a limited amount of time.

Hill Running: Hills are nature's way of reminding you that gravity still sucks. Running hills is the time-tested way to build endurance and leg strength. Find a short (75 to 100 yards) steep hill and attack it repeatedly. Run up the hill and jog down. Repeat 10 times or as many as you can do if 10 is impossible. If you do no other type of Intensity work, this should be the one to do.

Stadium Steps: Same approach and same benefits as hill running. Run up the bleacher steps, then jog down. Move over to the next aisle and repeat. Do as many as you can, but at least 30 minutes' worth.

Tempo runs: Know what your usual pace is? Well, do 10 to 20 minutes at a pace that's 30 seconds less and hold to this faster pace for the whole run. If your normal pace is about 9 minutes per mile, then crank it up so you do that same mile in 8:30. Tempo runs train your body to deal more efficiently with lactic acid build-up in your muscles. Lactic acid is what makes your muscles feel tired. Tempo runs are tough, but they make you tougher.

Fartlek: A Swedish term that means you alternate between your normal pace and a faster pace. Wearing a running watch during your usual running route, run hard for one minute, then slow down to your regular pace for a minute. Then speed up again. Alternate back and forth throughout your run.

Put on Some Weight: Put 10 pounds or so in a small backpack and wear it on your run. Cinch everything down tight so it doesn't bounce.

Sand, Snow, Trails: Running on irregular surfaces instead of on concrete or asphalt strengthens ankles and builds lower leg power.

Intervals: Running laps on a running track at close to your maximum level of effort is what makes speed work such a great tool for building strength . . . and such a meat-grinder. Speed work is tough. The typical work out will be sets of 400 (1 lap) or 800 meters (2 laps) followed by a jogging-speed recovery lap, followed by another set of laps at speed. Total distance isn't the goal; a fast pace that you can sustain for each repeat is what you're looking for.

No hills in your area? Find a local high school or sports stadium and run up the steps hard, then jog down. Repeat as often as you can.

July—and every condition in between. Weather is seldom a limiting factor for a serious runner. Unlike bicycling, another excellent aerobic conditioner, running doesn't let you coast downhill. Even if you slow to a walk, you're still exercising at a 400-calories/hour rate. Walking is good exercise in itself. The mechanical advantages of a bicycle mean you have to spend more time on a bicycle and focus harder on pushing yourself to get the same work out you'd achieve with a shorter run.

One Foot in Front of the Other

The reason too many people give up or avoid running has less to do with its difficulty than the fact that they're not doing it correctly. Like everything else, correct form has to be learned. It's one of those things that you'd think would come naturally, but it often has to be taught. It's not just putting one foot in front of the other, it's where you put that foot that makes the difference. If it lands in the wrong place, running will be harder, perhaps to the point of injury. More people would run and enjoy running if they understood how to do it correctly. Here are the rules:

• **Don't Bounce.** Many beginning runners spend as much time and energy going up as they do going forward. Wrong-o. Don't bounce. Direct your energy into going forward. You shouldn't be picking up your feet any more than necessary to take the next stride. If you look like a drum major leading a band, you're burning a lot of energy without going anywhere.

• **Run on Empty:** An empty stomach that is. At least two and preferably three hours after a meal is when you want to hit the road for your run.

• **Don't Overstride:** Running comfortably is about finding your natural and mechanically most efficient stride. Novice runners often take too-big steps, otherwise known as "overstriding." Take the Sock Test: While running, as your lead foot hits the ground, look down. If your foot is directly under your knee so you can't see your sock, your stride is correct. If it's ahead of your knee, what

Your heart is your body's most important muscle. Like most muscles, it responds to strenuous use by adapting and becoming stronger. Bicycling is one of several types of aerobic exercise you need to put on your workout menu if you want a stronger heart and lungs. *istock.com*

you're doing is like hitting the brakes every time you take a step. You're over-striding if you can see your sock.

• **Heel First.** The only time you run on the balls (front) of your feet is when you're sprinting at maximum speed. You can only do this for a brief period of time and that's the way Mom Nature meant it to be. For any kind of distance running, your feet should always land heel-first and then pivot up to the ball of your foot to launch you forward into the next step. Yes, you can train yourself to run properly. It may take a few weeks of conscious effort, but in time your form will adjust. The balls of your feet weren't intended to take a pounding and runners who persist in running in this way are the ones who spend most of their time injured. Plant

that heel first, and then let the miles pile up.

• **Heads Up!** Proper running form means good posture. You should look like you've got a steel rod inserted in your spine, not a Slinky. Don't slouch! Get that head up and fix your eyes on that distant, beautiful horizon you're running toward. Breathe deep with your shoulders back, and you'll be running efficiently. You will also have a slightly longer stride, which is better to cover those miles.

• **Relax.** Yeah, I know I just told you to stand up straight, but that does-n't mean you have to look like a Marine during inspection. Good posture, yes, but rigid and inflexible, no. Your shoulders and upper arms should be relaxed and swinging freely directly above your

hips. Don't lock your arms. They should swing along, flexed at about 90 degrees and close to your body. Your hands shouldn't be clenched tight, but they also shouldn't flop around. Your movements should be fluid like a well-oiled machine, which is what you're becoming. Spend your energy on covering ground efficiently. Just like on your motocross bike, you want to flow over the ground using the least energy while maintaining the maximum speed.

• **Warm Up and Cool Down.** You wouldn't try to grab the holeshot with the choke still on, and you need to give your body the same chance to warm up. Before heading out on your run, do a 5-minute warm-up routine by jumping rope, peddling a stationary bike, or just start walking briskly. The idea is to get

BUILD UP BEFORE RACE SEASON

Because endurance training takes a lot out of you, it's generally counterproductive to try do a lot of endurance during the main part of your racing season. It's too easy to end up worn out on race day. Instead, do your endurance training before the season starts, or before you get into the heart of the season. Then just run or bicycle enough to maintain your improved cardio level until season's end. Don't go looking for big jumps in your endurance strength unless you've got a lot of spare time, as otherwise the physical toll of training may affect your racing.

Yeah, this contradicts the "there is no off-season" advice, but unless you have unlimited spare time and buckets of commitment, it's hard to combine a tough cardio program, plus an ongoing strength program, with weekends devoted to racing. For every bit of training you do, you need recovery time or you won't see much progress. It can be tough to accept that your body requires time to recover in order to get stronger, but it's true. Try to squeeze in three days of intense cardio work and three days of strength training, plus a long day of racing, and pretty quickly you're either going to burn out or blow up. The exception to this is if you have no other job, school, or life commitments and can train daily for as long as necessary. If that's the case, go for it. The rest of us are envious.

Assuming that you're a normal guy with normal time limits and life stuff to deal with, it makes the most sense to do your time-eating cardio work outs before the race season gets underway. Work up to your cardio goal and then kick things into cruise to maintain your fitness level and get you through to race season's end.

Proper running form is something you have to learn and many people never do. Your arms should be at your side, your posture upright not leaning forward, and your feet should be landing heel first. You can learn and correct your running form. Do so and running will become simpler, easier and you'll be able to cover more distance with less effort.

your body up to operating temperature gradually, rather than all at once. Likewise, when you finish your run, don't just stop. Walk a bit more, do some push-ups or crunches, stretch again, and otherwise let your internal machinery spin down to normal rpm before you head for the shower.

Endurance Training to Lose Weight

Because endurance training burns more than 100 calories per mile (the exact amount depends on a host of factors), it's often recommended as the first-choice, sure-fire way to lose weight. Up to a point, that's true. Start running, bicycling, or cross-country skiing on a regular basis and you'll almost immediately see some weight loss. On average, running burns off 100 calories per mile, so if you get to where you're running 20 miles per week, that's 2,000 calories gone poof.

That's an impressive number, until you find out that losing a pound of body fat requires a 3,500 calorie deficit. Endurance training by itself may not be the best way to lose weight if that's your main reason for doing it. Running takes fat off your body but replaces it with muscle. That's why it's not unusual to actually gain weight as you start to work out on a regular basis, even as your clothes begin to fit better or feel more loose.

To lose your body's flabby tubes of goo, you need to combine endurance work outs with strength training, plus overhaul your diet. Some people think that by doing a lot of aerobic training it gives them a free ticket on the junk food train. But working out doesn't change the caloric equation. Your approach to fueling up your body each day is as important as your work outs in losing weight and keeping it off.

How to Know If You're Working Hard Enough

When you're training, how hard are you really working? Probably not as hard as you think.

Once you reach a certain point in your endurance training, running or bicycling at your usual pace isn't doing much except maintaining your current level of fitness and eating up your spare time. Just as with strength training, you have to increase the intensity to keep on getting stronger.

To get maximum results from your cardio work outs you must be training in your *target heart rate zone*, a percentage based on your Maximum Heart Rate (HRMax), which in turn is a general measure of your cardiovascular fitness. You calculate your HRMax by subtracting your age from 220. If you're 30 years old, your maximum heart rate (HRMax) would be 190. The only way to know for sure how many revs your heart is clocking is by wearing a heart rate monitor while you work out.

Running is the perfect exercise for most people, most times. Besides building cardio endurance, running lowers blood pressure, siphons off extra weight, requires almost nothing in equipment and can be performed 365 days of the year almost everywhere, no matter what the weather is like.

A heart rate monitor (HRM) provides a way to be sure you're working out as hard as you think you are or as hard as you should be. You want to work within a range of 70 to 85 percent of your maximum heart rate, a formula that matches age to physical fitness. See Chapter 9 for more details.

For the most bang from your aerobic work outs, train at 70 to 80 percent of your HRMax for 40 to 60 minutes a day, three or four times a week. Using the example of a 30-year-old's HRMax numbers of 190, that means training at a pace where the heart rate is in the 130 to 150 zone (70 to 80 percent of 190). You train most efficiently and see the greatest endurance-building results when you keep your heart rate within this target zone.

If weight loss is your main focus, then training at 60 to 70 percent of your HRMax (114 to 130, using the example above) is recommended. Again, this has to be for at least 40 minutes duration and three to four times a week.

Sounds great, right? Well, there's a catch you need to know about. The HRMax formula has a built-in flaw. Because it's an average, the HRMax formula doesn't work for people who regularly exercise at a high level. If you're already in very good shape, your target heart rate zone may be 20 to 30 points lower than what the formula says. Short of doing exhaustive testing, there's no easy way to establish what a very fit

If your area gets cold enough to have regular snowfalls, consider adding cross-country skiing to your training resume. It's an excellent cardio workout that's comparable to running and gives you one more reason to train outdoors no matter what the season is. *istock.com*

A heart rate monitor is nothing more than an electronic nag, a way to ensure you're training at the proper level. The monitors consist of an elastic chest strap containing the wireless transmitter, and a running watch that receives the information from the transmitter. There aren't any wires and you'll hardly notice you have it on.

Do you need one? Yes and no. You can certainly train without one, plus, as I've explained, if you're already extremely fit, the standard formula for calculating your HRMax doesn't apply. So, if you're a stubborn SOB and are good at pushing yourself along at a hard pace, you can do without a heart rate monitor. If, however, you're like most people and need a nudge and some nagging to remind you to work as hard as you should, then a heart rate monitor will help you do so.

How Far to Run

Distance is good and more distance is better, but only up to a point. Runners tend to make too big a deal out of how many miles they log, just as weight lifters focus on how many pounds they can bench press. The number of miles person's HRMax really is. If you fall into this category, then you're probably also in touch with what your body can and can't do and you know when you're working at high intensity. For this reason, heart rate monitors are often most useful for people at the beginning and intermediate stages of aerobic training. Elite athletes rely on them more to fine-tune and build up to a peak level in preparation for a specific race than as a general cardio training reminder.

TAKE WALK BREAKS

If you find your internal engine bouncing off the rev limiter while running, slow things down to a brisk walk. Walk breaks help you complete your total distance and you're still burning calories at a high rate, about half that of running. A few minutes spent walking will recharge you so you can crank the motor back up to running speed. Many people think that if you're going to run, slowing to a walk is cheating. That's just not true. In fact, many marathon training programs recommend walking breaks as a way to successfully finish a long training run or the marathon itself.

You race on hot, humid days. So your training should be under similar conditions. Your body needs to learn how to deal with heat and humidity while exercising so it can adapt. People who do all their aerobic workouts in the cool of morning are missing out on a chance to be stronger on race day.

same distance each time. You'll just run a little slower for a longer time (if you hear a serious runner mentioning LSD—long slow distance—this is what he's talking about).

So how far should you run? There's no fits-all answer to that, but threaten me with being force-fed a fried Twinkie and the number I'll throw out is "20 miles per week." It's an easy-to-remember goal and easy to slot into your training calendar because it can be divided by 4 or 5 days of the week. Twenty miles is also a distance that a runner with an established base can do easily, week in and week out, to maintain their fitness level.

But it's just a number and since your focus is on becoming a better motocross racer, not lowering your 10K times, it's not an important one. What you want is running that builds strength and endurance that you can put to use controlling that 450cc bucking monster between your legs.

Before you can answer the "how much distance?" question, you need to determine where you are in terms of cardiovascular strength. Keep reading . . . .

Novice, Intermediate, or Expert?

Endurance training is a lot like sign-up at a motocross. Your abilities determine where you fit into the big picture: You're either a Novice, Intermediate, or Expert. Back in Chapter 3, I had you conduct a cardio test by running six laps (approximately 1.5 miles) on a running track. If you haven't yet done that test, do it now (and see Chapter 3 for instructions). If you did the test, enter your results in the space below:

1.5-mile run time: _____

Your 1.5-mile run time provides a quick and reasonably accurate picture of your current cardiovascular fitness level. Here's what the times tell you:

You're a **Novice** if your time was over 14 minutes (15 minutes if you're 40 years old).

you pound out is seen as some indication of results, but that's not an accurate picture.

Here's another piece of basic exercise math for you: Aerobic conditioning is a combination of distance plus intensity. You can run a very long distance at low intensity, yet get only half the benefits you'd receive if you spent less time at a higher level of effort (intensity).

Intensity comes in different flavors. Hills add intensity as does speed work

(running fast laps) on a track. Tempo runs are an easy way to add intensity to your work out. A tempo run is simply breaking up the run into sections, some run at your normal pace, and others at higher speed, then returning to your normal pace. You do this throughout the run.

Once you've established a solid running base, distance becomes the least effective way to add intensity. A few more miles simply aren't going to make much difference in your overall fitness if you're already doing about the

You're an **Intermediate** if your time was between 12 and 14 minutes.

You're an **Expert** if your time was between 9 and 12 minutes.

The sections that follow are running-based cardio programs appropriate for each level. The training listed here covers an eight-week period, which is a good minimum buildup period prior to the racing season. It's not a magic number, however, so if you have more time before the season starts, adapt the plan to a longer training schedule.

If there's a physical reason why you cannot run, adjust the times and mileage in this manner for other forms of aerobic work outs:

• Bicycling (road): Increase distances and times by at least one-third.

• Swimming: 8 minutes of swimming laps is equivalent to one mile of running.

• XC skiing: no adjustment necessary.

Your running work outs are going to require four types of running routes:

1. One flat route, but don't use a running track because you'll quickly bore yourself to death.

2. A moderately hilly (rolling hills, not mountains) route.

3. A high school or college running track.

4. Stadium steps like you'd find at the running track, or as an alternative, a steep hill approximately 75 to 100 yards long. The hill can be a grassy hillside in a park or a sidewalk. The grassy hillside is easier on your knees, especially coming down.

If you've never run or trained in any real way, it doesn't matter what your 1.5-mile test time was, you need to start at the Novice level and get a solid aerobic base established first. Also, keep in mind that there are a million different possible training programs out there. Modify this one as needed to get the aerobic results you want. This is a moderately ambitious training program, even at the Novice level, but if it's still too much, then fine-tune it to fit your needs. Drop down a level (go from

Run hills! Hills build strong legs and make you tougher. Doing repeats on a steep hill is a killer excercise, but produces great strength gains.

Intermediate to Novice, for example) and follow that program instead, or if you're in the Novice group, drop the mileage total down by a couple miles and follow the program for 12 weeks instead of 8 weeks.

Also, don't overdo things. Getting results from endurance training takes time, but Americans are always impatient. Resist the temptation to start out at the Expert level and blitz a series of six-mile runs, thinking you can force your body to develop a high level of cardiovascular endurance in a matter of days. It won't happen.

The Novice
You probably wheezed through your 1.5-mile timed test and maybe couldn't even cover the whole distance. You're pretty much starting from zero here.

Well, everybody has to start from somewhere, so don't let it get you down. The beauty of cardio training is that you start to see results very quickly. The people to feel sorry for are the ones who are already in such good shape that any measurable improvement is going to require prodigious levels of effort.

Set aside three days per week on alternating days (Monday-Wednesday-

SMALL STEPS

Pressed for time and you can only notch three miles of running on four or five days a week? Think it's not worth the bother? Wrong-o! Studies show that even 10 minutes of intense aerobic exercise a day is beneficial and produces noticeable improvements. A three-mile run done five times a week adds up to over 800 miles per year.

Running tracks provide another way to add intensity. Serious runners call this "speed work" because just like hills, this builds both physical and mental strength and toughness. Alternate laps, doing one hard, one at a jog, for the full distance you've got scheduled for that day. Most high school tracks these days are measured in meters and 4 laps will equal about a mile.

Friday, for example) for your endurance training. You'll be able to do most of these work outs in 45 minutes to an hour. Do at least a 5-minute warm-up of some type, including some light stretching. Jumping rope is a good warm-up. Follow this training schedule:

Week One: Three miles per work out on flat terrain. Or if that's too difficult, start at two miles. Run at a pace you can maintain for the whole distance, or for most of it. Walk as necessary in order to complete the distance. If you can't run even 2 miles, then walk it.

Week Two: Same as Week One, except try to keep the walking minimal or eliminate it completely.

Week Three: Switch to your hilly running route, keeping the mileage the same. None of the hills should be more than a quarter-mile in length. You want gently rolling terrain, not the High Sierras. Again, if you can't run the entire distance, take walk breaks so you still get your total distance.

Week Four: Same as Week Three, still on the hilly route so you're building some strength into your quads. By now you should be able to run the whole distance or getting pretty close to it. The same rule applies: walk as necessary in order to hit your mileage totals.

Week Five: Time to bump up the mileage. Add a mile to each work out, for a 4-mile total. Do two of the work outs on your flat route and one on your hilly trail.

Week Six: Same as Week Five, except do all your work outs on the hilly route.

Week Seven: By now you should be noticeably stronger and able to run at a comfortable pace. I bet you've noticed some weight loss, you're no longer short of breath, and if you check your resting pulse rate, it's probably gotten noticeably lower—all good stuff.

Week Eight: Same as Week Seven, except spend one day doing one of the intensity work outs (see the sidebar on page 60) to built speed and strength. At the end of Week Eight, you will have covered approximately 80 miles and established a solid endurance fitness base. After this week, you can choose to follow the Intermediate Endurance Schedule or maintain this level of training as the race season gets underway.

The Intermediate

You're in at least average condition as demonstrated by your 1.5-mile test time. In fact, you might be able to achieve this time without doing any actual training. An average-shape 20-year-old male can run 1.5 miles in a mid-11 to mid-12 minute time, so your time is neither wonderful nor awful, just average. But who wants to be average?

You'll start this program with work outs on three alternating days in the beginning, but graduate to a four-day schedule in Week Seven. In most cases, your work out will be complete and you'll be in the shower in just over an hour. Before your runs, do at least a 5-minute warm-up of light stretches, jumping rope, push-ups, or other exercises that will get your heart pumping at a faster pace.

Follow this training schedule:

Week One: Three work outs during the week, 4 miles per work out on relatively flat terrain. Take walking breaks as necessary in order to complete the distance, but on most days you should be able to run the whole distance. Maintain a comfortable pace, but also push yourself to finish the run without walking.

Having a training partner, whatever the sport, makes work outs easier to do. Besides the companionship, a training partner helps you stick to your work out schedule. Some days your partner will be dragging you out of the house; other days you'll be doing the honors.

Week Two: Same as Week One. Spend two days on your hilly training route and only one day on your flat route. Hills build your quads and your lungs, besides being a personal gut check you shouldn't skip.

Week Three: Same as Week Two.

Week Four: Add a mile to your work out, bumping it up to 5 miles, three times a week. Do all three runs on your hilly route. If you're feeling ambitious, schedule a fourth day of running, doing one of the intensity drills.

Week Five: Same as Week Four, 5 miles per run.

Week Six: Halfway through the program, and it's going to be a busy week. Spend one day at the local running track, doing five miles (20 laps) total. Do a lap fast (at 70 percent or more of your HRMax if you have a heart rate monitor), then a lap at a more comfortable cruising pace, so you end up doing 10

ON-ON!

Hate running by yourself? Want running to be more fun? The answer may lie with a worldwide group called the Hash House Harriers. This is an uncompetitive and very informal group of runners (adults only, sorry kids) who meet to follow a trail laid by "the hare" that can literally go anywhere. Along the way are beer stops and other amusements. "Hashers," as they're called, have groups in nearly every city in the world. There are no dues, no membership fees, and no requirements other than showing up ready to run and a sense of humor. I have been a hasher for more than 15 years and highly recommends it as a cure for work out boredom. To find a group in your area, log on to www.half-mind.com.

laps at speed and 10 laps cruising. Alternate back and forth each lap. On your fast laps, do *not* go at an all-out sprint, but you should be pushing hard with just a little left in reserve. If you're not using a heart rate monitor, use a stop watch or runner's watch to clock your lap times. Do an easy warm-up lap or two before you start and another cooldown lap when you finish (no, these don't count against your 20-lap total). Do two other runs of 5-mile length on your hilly running route.

Week Seven: You've got a decent distance endurance base in place now, so the only way to see some real gains is to add intensity, not distance. Schedule four work outs for this week. Two of them will be intensity work outs and two will be regular 5-mile runs on your hilly route. One of the two intensity work outs should be either the Stadium Steps or Hill Work outs. The second

intensity work out can be any of the others, your choice.

Week Eight: Same as Week Seven. At the end of Week Eight, you will have covered approximately 120 miles and established a respectable endurance fitness level. After this week, you can choose to follow the Expert endurance schedule or just repeat this program to maintain and build on this level of training as the race season gets underway.

The Expert

Based on your 1.5-mile test time, you're in pretty good shape. Your reward, you lucky dog, is having to work harder to see any significant improvement. This means booking some serious work out time, so your social life may suffer a bit. You're going to need to set aside four days per week for your endurance training and two days for your strength work

outs. And before you head out to do your runs, first do at least a 5-minute warm-up of some type, including some light stretching. Jumping rope is good. Follow this training schedule:

Week One: Three runs of five miles each on a hilly route at a steady but comfortable pace. You must be able to finish this distance without having to walk. If you can't complete the run without having to walk, you need to do the Intermediate Training routine instead.

Week Two: This starts your four-day training schedule. Spend three days on your hilly route, running the whole 5-mile distance. Spend one day doing one of the Intensity work outs of your choice.

Week Three: Add a mile to your work outs, bumping it up to 6 miles. Two of these work outs will be Intensity sessions and two will be your usual distance runs on your hilly route. For the Intensity work outs, one will be on the running track and one will require short, steep hills or stadium steps.

Spend one day at the local running track, doing six miles (24 laps) total. Do a lap fast (at 70 percent or more of your HRMax if you have a heart rate monitor), then a lap at a comfortable cruising pace, so you end up doing 12 laps at speed and 12 laps cruising. Alternate back and forth each lap. On your fast laps, do NOT go at an all-out sprint, but you should be pushing hard with a little left in reserve. If you're not using a heart rate monitor, use a stop watch or runner's watch to clock your lap times. Do an easy warm-up lap or two before you start and another cool-down lap when you finish (no, these don't count against your 24-lap total).

The second Intensity work out will be 45 minutes of either Stadium Steps [see the sidebar for how these are done] or the Hill Work outs [ditto]. Schedule at least one day of no running between your two Intensity sessions.

Week Four: Same as Week Three. Yeah, it's tough. It's supposed to be.

Endurance training is tough and it's easy to find a reason to quit. Don't. 'Nuff said. *istock.com*

Week Five: A change of pace is needed, so this week we cut back to three work outs. However, one of them is going to be a long run in order to boost your overall endurance. Schedule one long run work out of 8 to 10 miles,

depending on time available and how difficult you find the added distance. Make this the second or third work out of the week, not the first. For the other two work outs, do one Intensity session of your choice and one regular (6-mile) distance run on your hilly running route.

Week Six: Repeat the Week Four schedule with four work outs.

Week Seven: Repeat the Week Five schedule with three work outs, one of which is a long run of 8 to 10 miles. We're intentionally making some weeks harder and others easier. Remember that recovery time is an important part of your training.

Week Eight: Four work outs this week: One long run of 8 to 10 miles; one 6-mile run on your hilly course; and the two Intensity work outs of fast laps and hills as in Week Seven. At the end of Week Eight, you will have covered approximately 170 miles and added significant endurance. After completing this week, you can choose to follow the Intermediate Endurance Schedule with its shorter, three-day schedule to maintain this level of training as the race season gets underway.

TWO-MINUTE BOARD

- Endurance training is for the biggest, most important muscle in your body: your heart.
- This is the training that separates the men from the boys. It's easy to wimp out.
- Everybody thinks they know how to run, but a lot of people do it wrong.
- Use a heart rate monitor to make sure you're working as hard as you think you are and as hard as you need to.
- Do six laps (1.5 miles) on a running track and record the time to determine your cardiovascular fitness.
- Don't just do the same run every day. You have to have variations that add intensity in order to see any gains.
- Try to do the bulk of your cardio training build-up before the race season starts.

Chapter 7

BUILDING MOTO MUSCLE

You need a lot of strength to race motocross. Yet, as odd as it may sound, you don't need or even want big muscles.

Don't believe it? Well, take a look at any of the top pros when they have their shirts off. They're obviously very fit and trim, but you don't see the rippling abs and bulging biceps of muscle-magazine cover models. If you didn't already know who they were and what they do for a living, you wouldn't be able to guess from their physiques alone. A top rider's physique is trim and fit, not heavily muscled. Muscle size and mass does matter, but in the opposite sense than you might expect.

While lifting weights seems pretty simple and obvious, if you want to see specific results as quickly as possible, you have to understand a few not-so-obvious facts.

Building Strength

The four basics of any strength-training program are these:

1. Resistance (the amount of weight)
2. Repetitions (how many you do)
3. Sets (the number of repetitions you do in one continuous attempt = one set)
4. Rest (how long you let the muscles recover between sets)

Just like baking a cake, you mix and adjust these four strength-training ingredients to get what you need:

If You Want Strength:
Resistance: Heavy
Repetitions: 3 to 8
Sets: 3 to 5
Rest: 2 to 5 minutes between sets

Strength comes from moving mass quantities of steel up and down. There's no escaping this little fact.

If You Want Size:
> Resistance: Moderate
> Repetitions: 8 to 12
> Sets: 3 to 5
> Rest: 30 to 90 seconds between sets

If You Want Muscle Tone (how the muscles and your body look):
> Resistance: Light
> Repetitions: 12 to 20
> Sets: 2 to 3
> Rest: 20 to 30 seconds between sets

Muscle is dense and heavy and having too much of it usually makes you less flexible. For motocross-specific training, we want strength and endurance without the bulk. That means using weights that are close to your maximum ability to lift, doing fewer repetitions, and aiming for three to five sets with two- to five-minute rests between sets. This is how you build moto-muscle strength instead of body-builder bulk.

What's with This Rest Stuff?

When trainers talk about rest, they don't mean sitting on your butt in front of the TV with a cold beer at hand. While it seems contrary to what you're trying to accomplish, training requires both longer and shorter periods of rest to obtain the benefits you're after. It's not just a case of working nonstop to the point of passing out from exhaustion. The longer you work a muscle continuously, the less benefit and strength you'll get.

Exercise doesn't actually build muscles; exercise tears muscles down. Then your body goes to work repairing the damage to make the muscle better than it was before. Basically, you're overloading your muscles so they'll adapt to the stress and come back bigger and stronger.

Rest and recovery come in both long- and short-term flavors. You're probably familiar with the idea that you shouldn't weight-train the same muscles two days in a row. You need to allow at least a day between so that they can recover. That's long-term rest. However, the short-term rest between sets is also a critical factor that determines the effects of the work out.

For building moto-specific muscle, where your goal is strength without bulk, the rest between sets should be two to five minutes. The longer you rest between sets, the more your muscles recover and the harder you'll be able to push them in the next set of reps.

Strength Training For Beginners

Sad to say, but the reason many people never stick to a weight training program is that they don't know where to begin or what to do. Here's the basics if you're a complete novice and it's good information even if you think you know your way around a gym:

Start with One Set: It's silly to go from doing zero weightlifting sets to busting a gut trying to do three sets of some exercise you've never done before. Instead, spend your first few weeks doing just one set of each of the exercises. This gives your muscles, joints and tendons time to adjust to the new demands.

Start Light: Use a weight for each exercise that's going to seem too light. It should be a weight that you can lift for 15 repetitions, even though you're going to stop at 6 or 8 reps when you actually do the exercise.

Alternate Days: Don't work the same muscles on a daily basis. Your body builds muscles during the recovery period, not when you're actually lifting the weight. Two strength work outs per week are plenty.

Think Big First: Major areas of the body—chest, back, legs, arms—aren't individual muscles, but muscle groups. You should always work the big muscle groups first, leaving smaller individual muscles like the biceps and triceps for last. If you do it the opposite way, doing single-muscle exercises first, you will fatigue them and they won't be up to the job when you need them for the big muscle group exercises.

Go Slow: Rapid movements strain muscles and tendons. Be slow but steady, especially while lowering the weight.

Focus on Form: It's not just how much weight you lift, but how you do it. Perform an exercise wrong by doing things like arching your back or jerking the weight around and you're wasting your time. You also increase your chances of getting hurt. Focus on learning and using the proper form for each exercise, rather than getting stuck on how much weight you're pushing. Study the pictures and always pay attention to your form.

Cut Loose in Three Weeks: If you follow the above advice, by the start of the third week you should be ready to do multiple sets and lift heavier weights.

Too Much Advice

Keep in mind that the body has hundreds of muscles, and there are at least that many different ways to approach strength training. There are hundreds of different strength-training programs out there, and thousands of coaches and gyms with their own "guaranteed success" approaches. You could easily devote every waking hour of every day to trying all the different exercises to be found in magazines, books, and online.

What you need is a simple program that works the main muscles called upon

10 REASONS TO LIFT WEIGHTS

1. You'll lose fat faster, when combined with a healthy diet and cardiovascular exercise.
2. You'll feel stronger and more fit.
3. You'll have more energy.
4. Your back will be stronger and less likely to bother you.
5. You'll have more functional strength for daily chores, your job, other sports, and, of course, racing.
6. Your bones will become stronger.
7. You can do most strength training at home with minimal investment in equipment.
8. It's not boring, especially if you change your training routine every 3 or 4 weeks.
9. Getting stronger makes you more confident . . . in everything.
10. You'll get visible results.

while racing a motorcycle. A program that is doable without forcing you to live at the gym in order to follow it.

Work, Damnit!

If you want results, you have to work. Instead, most people do the same exact work out every single time. That's not going to cut it.

Remember, we're humans and genetically programmed to be as lazy as overfed poodles. The body doesn't like to work. So what we tend to do at the gym is perform the exact same exercises with the exact same intensity, for months (or years!) on end. Technically we're working out, but what we're really doing is coasting.

If you want to see results and steady improvement from your strength and aerobic training, you have to *work*. That means sweat, effort, and high intensity all leading up to that wonderful totally wasted feeling where your muscles are burning and exhausted, your work out clothes are soaked in sweat, and you've got nothing left.

Change Your Routine

The typical training routine described here and in most programs will consist of 6 to 10 specific exercises. It's easy to focus on doing those exercises and nothing more, but you shouldn't. Doing the same things all the time gets you stuck in a training rut.

To avoid being stuck on a plateau, do this: Every three to four weeks, change your routine in some way. Add some new exercises while dropping others and change the amount of weight you're lifting, the number of reps, number of sets, or the rest period. Not only will making these changes offset work out boredom, but you'll be challenging your muscles in new ways—and that's a good thing. After a while, your body adapts to any type of stress and starts to coast along at part throttle. Changing your program once a month short-circuits this coasting and you'll get stronger, faster.

Bottom line: Don't do the same exercises all the time. Mix and match so that at least once a month you're adding something new to your routine, while dropping something else. As you become more accomplished and experienced with physical training, think of yourself as a student and every work out as a learning experience. Read other training books and subscribe to magazines focused on health, strength, and endurance. Talk to personal trainers and coaches or other racers who are training. Try new techniques and exercises. Learn what works for you and what doesn't.

How Often?

Unless you're trying to make the NFL (in which case, you've got the wrong book), in most cases, strength-training programs shouldn't be more than three

days of the week and two days is the norm. For an active racer, the typical training program in any given week will be three days of aerobic exercise, two days of strength training, a day of rest, and a day spent racing.

During the off-season, while preparing for a new racing season, it's okay to notch it up a level and spend six days in training and one day resting, alternating each day between endurance and strength work outs. However, training at that level of intensity is difficult for most people to maintain. Your body does need some down time, so a program of five days per week is a schedule that's easier to maintain.

Which Muscles?

There may be 650 muscles bunched together on your body, but we only care about these:

- Upper body (chest, upper back, and shoulders)
- Abdominals
- Lower back
- Forearms and upper arms
- The big leg muscles: quadriceps, hamstrings, calves

The exercises pictured on the next few pages focus on these areas. Just to repeat myself, we're looking to build strength and not to turn you into someone with an underwear model's ripped physique. If your main goal is to have six-pack abs and bulging biceps so you can wow the babes at the beach, you've got the wrong book. We're going to build functional strength for moto.

Find Your 1RMax

"1RM" is training lingo for your "One Rep Maximum." This is the maximum weight you can lift with proper form, one time. Note the "proper form" aspect. You have to do the lift correctly; jerking the weight up in a desperate attempt to do the exercise in any way you can manage doesn't count and is an invitation to injury.

You should establish what your 1RM is for each exercise, so you can

WHAT'S MY ONE-REP MAX?

One-rep max (1RM) is the most weight you can lift once, with good form, no cheating, no arched back. Ideally, you train with weights that are 60 to 70 percent of your 1RM. Sounds good, but how do you figure out your 1RM without busting a gut or injuring yourself? Simple, use this chart and do a bench press, dead lift or military press to arrive at the numbers. The number of reps you can do at a certain weight will tell you how close you are to your 1RM.

Max Reps	1	2	3	4	5	6	7	8	9	10	12	15
% RM	100	95	93	90	87	85	83	80	77	75	67	65
Weight lifted (lbs or KG)	200	190	186	180	174	170	166	160	154	150	134	130

Shoulder Shrug

Shoulder shrugs build up those all-important shoulders while also protecting your rotator cuff. With a dumbbell in either hand, arms at your sides, shrug your shoulders up as if you were trying to touch your ears with your shoulders.

then train at 60 to 75 percent of your 1RM. Training at that level means you are working at the most effective level for building strength.

The Plan

With, quite literally, hundreds of potential exercises to do, how do you choose?

Keep it simple. Choose two to three of these strength building exercises from each of the body area categories (upper body, abs, etc.), and do them for at least one month. At the end of the month, change a few of the exercises by adjusting either the number of sets or the exercise itself.

Your work out plan then should have between 10 and 15 strength-training routines which will take you 60 to 90 minutes to complete. Devote at least 10 minutes before you begin your strength routines to doing the Core Exercises listed in Chapter 4. The Core Exercises do double-duty as a warm-up, while at the same time delivering real benefits you don't want to miss.

Finally, don't forget the rest portion of your work out. If you're trying to build strength, there should be from 2 to 5 minutes between sets.

Upper Body: Chest, Upper Back, Shoulders

These three distinctly different muscle groups are lumped together because the exercises are similar with only slight variations and because there's too much focus on building the chest and shoulders, and not nearly enough attention paid to the equally important upper back. Ignore your upper back at your own risk, because a strong back is your anchor for the rest of your physique.

Shoulder Shrugs: Holding a pair of dumbbells at your sides, try to touch your shoulders to your ears by shrugging. You won't actually touch your ears, of course, but that's the easiest way to describe the movement. Keep your back straight and your head up. Do two to three sets of six to eight reps.

Bench Press: Grab the bar with your hands just wider than shoulder width. Hold the bar over your chest at arm's length and then slowly lower the bar to just above your chest. Pause and then push it straight up to the starting position. Do two to three sets of six to eight reps.

WORST TIME TO WORK OUT?

You're at your physical worst, with reaction times and endurance at their lowest ebb (by 50 percent or more), after 17 to 19 hours of being awake. In other words, toward the end of a normal day. Do I need to tell you that this is also the worst time of day to try and train?

Bench Press

The bench press is an exercise you can't skip, but it also shouldn't be the whole focus of your weight training routine. As always when doing these, keep your back flat on the bench, don't let it arch, and if you're pushing a lot of weight, have a spotter.

Bench Press Variations: There are several variations to the basic bench press that add intensity: 1. Put your hands closer to the center of the bar; 2. Put your hands further apart (wide-grip) on the bar; 3. Incline the bench and use either the barbell or two dumbbells.

Dumbbell Flies: Lie on your back on a bench with your feet firmly on the floor and a light dumbbell in each hand. Hold the dumbbells directly above you, palms facing each other. Slowly lower the dumbbells out and away from each other, keeping your wrists locked. Lower until they reach chest level with

Inclined Bench Press

Close-Grip Bench Press

There are various ways to make the basic bench press more challenging and get some additional intensity. You can use a shorter bar, or place your hands either closer to the bar's center, or further apart than you normally would.

Adjust the bench to an inclined angle to create a more difficult bench press movement. You won't be able to muscle as much weight, but doing sets of these will build up your shoulders and upper back fast.

Dumbbell Flies

Dumbbell flies are arm and shoulder builders par excellent. Lying on a weight bench, arms outspread, bring them smoothly up. The action is if you're flapping your wings, trying to fly.

your elbows bent at about a 45-degree angle. Pause and then raise back to the starting position. Be sure your chest muscles are doing the work, not your shoulders. Do two to three sets of six to eight reps.

Lat Pull-Down: With a cable machine, attach the handlebar-like bar. Position yourself either standing or sitting, depending on the unit, and grab the bar with an overhand grip, arms shoulder-width apart. Pull the bar down to your chest, pause, and slowly return to the starting position. Do two to three sets of six to eight reps.

Lat Pull-down

Put the handlebar-style bar on the cable machine and pull down. Great shoulder-builder.

GET OUT THERE!

You lose your fitness two to three times faster than you acquire it. Suck it up, screw the excuses, shut off the damn TV, and get out there! Use it or lose it still applies.

Upright Row

Same as the lat pull-down, except this time you're lifting up. With both of these exercises, focus on keeping your back straight and letting your arms and shoulders do the work.

Upright Rows: Standing upright with a bar, hands close together in the center and palms facing in. Lift the bar to your upper chest. Pause and return to the start position. Keep your back straight and your head up.

Side Lateral Raises: Stand upright, arms at your sides, and hold a light dumbbell in each hand, palms facing your body. Raise both dumbbells straight out from your sides until they are at shoulder level. Pause, then lower. Do two to three sets of six to eight reps.

Side Lateral Raise

Build your triceps and reinforce those shoulder muscles with a side lateral raise. You'll have to use a relatively light weight to be able to do this one.

Prone Fly

If you have an exercise ball, you can do this variation of the side lateral raise. A prone fly is done with your chest on the exercise ball.

Shoulder Press

Need a little more work on your shoulders? Head for the shoulder press machine.

Shoulder Press: Grab a barbell with a grip that's just wider than shoulder-width. Stand holding the bar just above your chest, push the bar up until your arms are fully extended. Without pausing, slowly lower the bar back to your chest. Do two to three sets of six to eight reps.

Abdominals

Abdominal exercises are predominantly core routines with little or no equipment involved. However, an exercise ball, medicine ball, and weight plates can add a lot of intensity to your work out.

Ball Blaster: With a medicine ball or 5- to 15-pound weight plate, set an adjustable bench at a 45-degree angle. With the medicine ball or weight plate on your chest, sit up quickly and explosively, lifting the weight vertically until

Wood Chopper

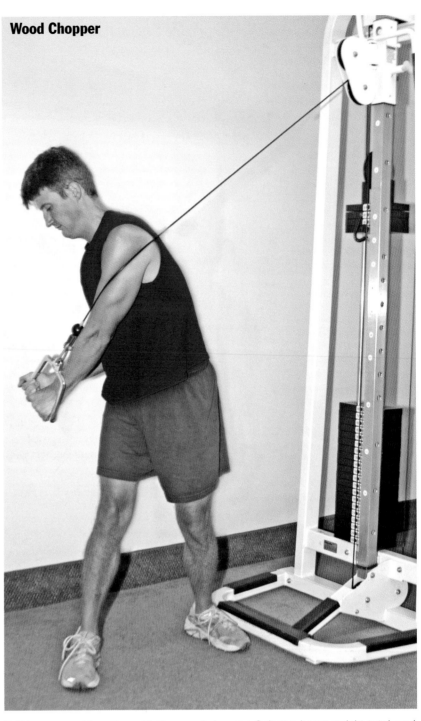

Build up your mid-section with the wood chopper. Select a heavy weight total, and with both hands holding the triangle, pull down and around, twisting your torso.

it's above your head. Keep your back flat. Because this is an advanced exercise, take it easy at first. Do one to two sets of six to eight reps.

Wood Chopper: At the cable machine, attach a stirrup handle and grab it with both hands. Stand with one side toward the cable and your feet shoulder-width apart. Pull the handle downward and diagonally across your body with both hands. Your shoulders should be rotating away from the cable machine. It's

THE REAL FAST FOOD

Forget the Golden Starches. If you want fast food that's really fast, then apples, grapes, carrots, bananas, peaches, plums, and other no-preparation fruits and vegetables are the quickest and best choices you can make. No standing in line on sticky floors waiting for greasy food; no worry about calories as these are nutrient-dense and water-rich foods; they are pre-packaged and may only require a quick washing; and cost-wise you're be ahead of the game in a big way.

Triceps Extension

as if you're chopping wood. Pause and slowly return. Because you're using two hands, set the weight stack to a relatively heavy setting. Do two to three sets of six to eight reps.

Weighted Crunches: Your basic crunch with added difficulty. When your regular crunch routine gets too easy, kick up the intensity by using a weight plate or medicine ball to increase the difficulty.

Lower Back
A strong lower back begins with a strong core and strong abs. These are the muscles that literally support your upper body.

Superman: This is a core exercise as detailed in Chapter 4, repeated here to remind you to be sure to do it. Lie on the floor, face down, with arms and legs extended. Raise your arms and legs off the floor so you look like Superman flying through the air. Hold for a count of 10. Do 2 to 3 sets of 10 reps. When this starts to get too easy, do more sets, more reps, or hold for a longer count.

Bird Dog: Starting on your hands and knees, extend one arm straight out in front of you and stretch the leg on the opposite side straight out behind you. Hold for a count of 10 and return to the start position. Switch arms and legs to work the other side. That's one set. Do a total of 10 sets or until you can't do any more.

Good Morning: Stand with your legs shoulder-width apart and with a light barbell on the back of your shoulders. Keeping your back level, slowly bend at the waist until your body is at roughly a 90-degree angle. Keep your

head up, your back straight, and knees slightly bent. Stop if you feel any pain. Do 2 to 3 sets of 6 to 10 reps.

Arms of Steel
You don't need to be Arnold or Popeye to know that strong arms are important.

Triceps Extension: Lie on your back on a bench with a pair of dumbbells. Hold the dumbbells with your arms straight up, angled toward your head. Your palms should be turned in toward each other. Without moving your upper arms, bend at the elbows and slowly lower the dumbbells as far as you can. Pause and return to the start position. Do two to three sets of six to eight reps.

Cable Curl

You can also use the cable machine for arm curls in all the usual variations.

With one dumbbell held with both hands behind your neck, lift up until it's just above your head (and make sure it doesn't slip!). Return to the start position and repeat.

Dumbbell Kickback

The dumbbell kickback is a triceps builder. Kneel on the bench, with one hand stabilizing your body. Curl the dumbbell backward and up, then return it to the start position (hanging by your side).

Cable Curls: Begin by facing the front of a cable pulley machine and stand 1 to 2 feet back. Start with the bar and cable down by your pelvis, then slowly curl up toward your chest. Pause, lower slowly, and repeat. Do two to three sets of six to eight reps.

Dumbbell Kickbacks: This really works your triceps, which are actually a bigger proportion of your arm muscles than the biceps. Hold a dumbbell in one hand, palm facing your body, and kneel with one leg on a bench. With the dumbbell at about chest height, straighten your arm out behind you and extend it until the arm is straight. Then return to the start position. Do two to three sets of six to eight reps per arm.

Wrist Extensions: Sit on a bench with your feet shoulder-width apart. Using a very light dumbbell in each hand, palms facing down, place your forearms on your thighs. Bend your

Concentration Curl

The concentration curl is another arm builder. One arm at a time, slowly curl the dumbbell up, your elbow resting on your knee. Do a set and then switch arms.

wrists to lower the dumbbells as far as possible. Next raise the weights as high as you can, keeping your forearms pressed against your thighs. Do two sets of six to eight reps.

Concentration Curl: Sitting on the edge of a bench with a dumbbell in one hand, rest that arm on the inside of your knee. Hold the weight with an underhand grip and let it hang straight down. Curl the weight up, pause, then lower the weight to the starting position. Do two to three sets of six to eight reps for each arm.

Wrist Curl

Wrist curls build stronger wrists and forearms. Support one arm with the other. Using a light dumbbell, curl it back and forth using only your wrist. Do 10 reps, switch hands.

Reverse Curl: Stand holding a barbell with a shoulder-width, overhand grip, and your arms hanging straight down. Keeping your back straight, slowly curl the bar up until your forearms touch your biceps. Pause, then slowly lower.

Wrist Roll-Ups: You either have to make this one or you can find manufactured versions in some sporting good stores. With a short piece of broom handle, pipe, or closet hanger rod, attach a 4-foot rope to one end and a weight plate to the other. With your arms held straight out in front of you,

Preacher Curl

The preacher curl builds your biceps and triceps (the triceps is the more important one). You can either do this either sitting on a regular bench or with a special bench that isolates the movement for more effect. Slowly curl the short bar up and down, while keeping your back straight.

roll the weight up using only your wrists. Not your shoulders or arms, just the wrists. Then slowly unroll it to return to the starting position. That's one set. Do 2 to 3 sets of 10 reps. You will definitely feel your wrists burning with this one.

Preacher Curl: Sitting at a preacher-curl station if available, grab a pair of light dumbbells or a short curl bar with an underhand grip. Rest your upper arms on the slanted pad. Keeping your back straight, slowly curl the bar or dumbbells up until your forearms are at a right angle to the floor. Then lower the weight back down. Do three sets of six to eight reps.

Hammer Curl: With a dumbbell in each hand, arms straight down at your sides, and palms facing in, slowly curl the dumbbells toward your shoulders. Your thumbs should be pointing to your shoulders at the end of the movement. Slowly lower to the starting position. Keep your back straight and be careful you're not using your shoulders or body weight to jerk the dumbbells up. The effort should be coming from your arms, not your shoulders. Do two to three sets of six to eight reps.

Big Wheels: Your Legs

Talk about work outs for your legs and most people think of aerobic training. Yes, you need that, but the muscle that primarily benefits from aerobic training is your heart, not your legs.

Dumbbell Squat: Start with a dumbbell in each hand, arms at your sides, and feet shoulder-width apart.

Hammer Curl

Slowly squat until your thighs are parallel to the floor, pause briefly, then straighten up and repeat. Keep your back straight.

Dead Lift: With the barbell resting on the floor, grip it with either an overhand grip (palms facing you) or an alternating grip (one palm facing you, one facing up). Straighten your legs and lift the barbell until you're upright. Remember that you're lifting with your legs, not your back. Then lower the bar to the start position. Do two to three sets of six to eight reps.

Leg Press: Position yourself in a leg-press machine so that your back and butt are flat against the seat. Your feet should be shoulder-width apart and at about a 45-degree angle. Slowly push the weight up away from you until your legs are straight, but your knees aren't locked (never lock your knees). Then slowly return to the start position. Do two to three sets of six to eight reps.

Dead Lift

Dumbbell Squat

The hammer curl is an arm blaster. With a dumbbell in each hand, alternately curl each arm up, using only your arms. Maintain good form and don't let your shoulders do the work.

Holding two dumbbells, do a front squat, keeping the dumbbells by your side. Return to the standing position and repeat as many times as you can. If you think the regular squat is a good work out, just try it with additional weight.

Deadlifts build your quads, and strengthen knees and lower back muscles. Using either a full-size barbell or a shorter bar (used here for photographic purposes) load the bar with a lot of steel. Squat in front of the bar, hands shoulder-width apart, and then stand straight up. All of the lift comes from your back and legs, none from your arms.

Leg Press

Spend some time every strength workout with the leg press to build your quads, abs, and groin muscles, as well as strengthen knees.

Calf Raises

Sitting on a bench, position two moderately heavy dumbbells on your knees, holding them in place. Keeping your toes on the floor, raise both legs using your calf muscles. Pause at the top, then return to the start position.

Seated Calf Raise: Sit on the edge of the bench with the balls of your feet on the floor. Place a dumbbell on each knee, holding it in place with your hands. Raise your heels by pushing down on the toes of your foot. Go as high as you can, then slowly lower toward the floor as far as you can. That's one rep. Do at least two sets of 8 to 10 reps.

Step-Up

Tougher than it looks, stepping up with a dumbbell in each hand will wear you out fast. Step up with one foot, then the other, then step back down, moving continuously. Adjust the box you're using to be a high step up for you, in order to get maximum effect.

Bench Step-Up: With a dumbbell in each hand, stand facing a flat bench. Step up quickly and plant one foot on the bench, then the other, and then step back down without pausing. It's like walking up the stairs, except with dumbbells in each hand. Do 2 sets of 15 reps.

FINDING A PERSONAL TRAINER

There are a lot of personal trainers out there and a lot of certification programs, so how do you find someone who's worth the hourly fee? Some advice:

· Before you spend a nickel, observe the trainer in action with other clients. Does he/she seem to have good rapport with them? Does he tailor the training to match the individual and their goals?

· Talk to them. Make sure they understand that your training goals are focused on a specific sport. They'll probably need to do some research or ask you a lot of questions to understand exactly what muscles are used in racing a motorcycle.

· See if they will agree to you buddying up to split the cost with another person and ask if they offer a trial session.

· Realize that a trainer, no matter how good he or she is, can't work miracles. You didn't become The Tower of Flab overnight and no trainer can transform you into a steely man of steel in just a few sessions.

· Decide on your own how often you need to meet with your trainer. Usually, the routine involves a lot of sessions at the beginning in order to get you pointed in the right direction, and then it tapers off to only occasional meetings where the trainer can evaluate your progress, answer your questions, and suggest new exercises.

· Don't be talked into signing any contracts until you're satisfied that the trainer is one you can live and work with comfortably.

Look for and use these two leg-muscle building machines. One exercises your quads (top) and the other (above) tackles those hard-to-work hamstrings.

Lunge

Lunges are part of your core workout, but by adding a dumbbell, you get a lot of leg strength quickly. From an upright standing position, lunge forward taking a long step, so your back leg is parallel to the floor, then powerfully step back to the start position. Pause briefly then step forward with the opposite leg and repeat.

Lunges: With a dumbbell in each hand, arms at your sides, and feet about 6 inches apart, step forward with one foot so your thigh is almost parallel to the floor. Keep your back straight. Stand back up and repeat the movement, but with the other foot. That's one rep. Do two to three sets of six to eight reps.

TWO-MINUTE BOARD

· You move a lot of steel in order to get a lot stronger. There's no better way to gain strength.

· To gain strength, you lift heavy weights a few times.

· Muscles get bigger during the resting stage, not when you're actually throwing the metal around.

· Change your routine regularly in order to avoid boredom and to let your muscles grow in new ways.

· Work! Most people don't try hard enough and just keep doing the same thing over and over.

· The goal isn't bulging muscles or six-pack abs to impress the girls, but strength and endurance that you can put to use on a motocross bike.

Chapter 8

FINDING TIME TO TRAIN

Unless you're independently wealthy or permanently unemployed, you've got a lot of built-in limits for how much time you can devote to training. The list is endless. School, work, kids, homework, the spouse or main squeeze, the commute, household chores, illness, vacation, trips, and of course the must-see TV intrusions. Heck, even the bike needs attention, which cuts another chunk out of your limited free time.

It's hardly any surprise that the number one excuse people cite for not exercising is "no time." This excuse is common in spite of the government's health recommendations for 30 to 90 minutes of exercise per day.

No time, you say? I don't believe it, so stop your whining. Even the busiest person out there has about 40 free hours per week. An excuse is exactly what the no-time claim really is. Working out is a matter of choice and *you* are the one who does or doesn't make the choice. Anybody can find an excuse to ditch a workout, because there are literally a million excuses available.

Your philosophy concerning training should be one of No Excuses Accepted. Or as Yoda said in *Star Wars*, "Do or not do. There is no try." Nike also got it right with the classic "Just Do It" campaign. Both messages should be part of your personal creed because both are life-changing philosophies worth taking to heart.

The bottom line is that everyone gets the same package of 24 hours a day. Some people use a chunk of that time to become and stay fit; others use those same hours to push the limits as elite, professional athletes; and lots of others use it to put a permanent dent in their sofa. It's your choice.

How Much Time?

To train effectively for any sport, one hour per day for five days a week should be your absolute minimum commitment. Twice that amount—ten hours a week—is better. Note that this doesn't include any riding time on your dirt bike, which is why you're logging the hours in the first place.

Does it sound like too much time? Well, to put it in perspective, the average American watches about 30 hours of

Everybody starts with the same 24 hours. You set aside time for work, school, favorite TV shows, evenings out, parties, and other events. Well, you do the same thing with workouts. Block out some time on your schedule and show up, ready to sweat.

Some weeks it seems like you barely have the time to race, let alone train. So how do you find the time to do your work outs? You make the time, just as you make appointments for other things in your busy, busy life.

television each week. If you can find the time to put your brain in neutral and watch the tube, you can just as easily choose to do something active instead.

Sixty minutes a day really isn't much, but if even that commitment is too heavy on some days (and we all have those kind of days), here's a thought: If you can't find a free hour, then do at least 20 minutes of high-intensity aerobic exercise and you'll get most of the physical benefits of a longer work out. The key words are "high intensity."

When you're short of time, that's a cue to ramp up the intensity of what you're doing. Instead of running five miles at your normal steady pace, sprint three miles as hard as you can do them. Or switch from training on a flat course to doing hills. Go to the nearest high school football field and run the bleacher steps. If you're in the gym, focus on strength training routines that work a lot of muscles hard: the squat, dead lift, bench press, lat pull-down, and shoulder press.

The rule is always the same: When you're short of time, increase the intensity to maximize the results of your work out.

Finding Hidden Extra Time

Assuming your options don't include quitting your job or school and training full-time, you need to take a hard look at your daily schedule and figure out what's important and what's not. There are a lot of wasted extra hours you can tap into, if you choose to. Some possibilities:

THE CALENDAR APPROACH

Making sure you have time for your work out can be as simple as putting it promi-
nently on your office desk or wall calendar. Besides being a reminder to you that
you have an appointment with yourself, you can point at it when some coworker wants
you to work late on the latest rush project. "Sorry dude, I've already got that time
booked up."

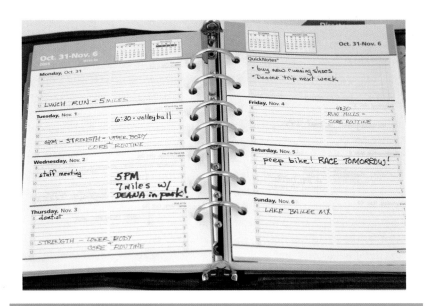

• Work out in front of the TV. The
biggest time-eater of them all can actually
become part of your training routine and
help you get through a work out. Put a
set of dumbbells nearby or do your work
out in a gym where TVs crowd every
wall. Riding an exercise bike while
watching the boob tube is an excellent
approach (although, personally, I prefer
to read while on the bike). Use commercial breaks to do push-ups, sit-ups,
crunches, and other core muscle-building
exercises that require no equipment and
just a flat piece of floor. The one or two
minutes of commercial time are wasted
minutes anyhow.

• Work out at lunch. While everyone else is loading up on calories, you
can be burning them. An added benefit
is that your energy levels will be higher
in the afternoon and your evenings will
be free for chores, errands, another
work out, or some serious garage time
with your favorite two-wheeler.

• Commute using your muscles. If
feasible, walk, run, or bicycle to work or
school. I have a racing buddy who regularly commutes to his office by bicycle,
for a 15–mile ride each way. He manages
to beat most of the rush hour crowd
that's traveling the same distance by car,
since he can take less-crowded streets and
doesn't ever get caught in gridlock.

• Simplify your work out. The more
complicated it is, the more impediments
you have to doing it, and probably the
more time it requires. Instead of doing
three sets of each weight repetition, do
two sets. Instead of running seven miles,
run six. Instead of committing to an
overly demanding work out and then
finding an excuse to duck it because you
don't have the time, change the work out
to match the time you do have.

• Gym time is for your work out,
not socializing or warming up. Are you
really using what time you do have?
Health clubs are a hot dating scene, as

you've probably noticed. Watch the
crowd at the typical health club, and
you'll see two things: a lot of socializing
going on, and a lot of people who spend
15 minutes warming up, followed by
maybe 10 minutes of actually working
out, before they start their cool-down
and stretches.

• Cross-train. To achieve lifelong
fitness, expand your interests. There are
days when it makes perfect sense to play
hooky, ducking the gym and your
planned work out, to do something else.
That something else should be another
active sport that works your muscles,
causes you to sweat, and raises your
heart rate. Things like taking a leisurely
bicycle ride, volleyball (especially sandpit
or beach versions), basketball, soccer,
cross-country skiing, hockey, inline
skating, or tennis are all great alternatives. If you're still in school, go out for
a sport. Even if you eventually don't
make the team, the conditioning period
leading up to the tryouts can be invalu-
able. Again, it has to be something
active and not a game like golf. By having
some cross-training alternatives, you
have a pressure release from times when
your work out plan has become stale
and boring. Better to do something
active than use your boredom as an
excuse to not do anything at all.

• Make a date with yourself. Block
out the time for a week ahead or more on
your daily planner. Better yet, mark your
work out appointments on one of those
big wall calendars, which will make it
harder to miss. Make it an appointment,
just like all the other appointments you
have every week. Just as you can't skip an
appointment with your boss, teacher, or
dentist without repercussions, you
shouldn't miss a work out appointment.
For a lot of people, treating their work
outs as a must-do appointment is easier
than any other approach.

• Get a training partner. It's not
that the partner is going to manufacture time for the both of you, but having someone else who expects you to
be there has a magical effect. There will
be days when you'll be the one nagging
your partner to be on time; then there

People are always looking for excuses to get out of their training appointment. Except in rare cases, the weather should never be an excuse. Dress properly and you can train outdoors in almost any weather Mom Nature can throw at you. The author has run on days when the temperatures were far below zero and days when it was well over 100 degrees. It isn't always fun, but what you learn is that weather can't stop you.

will be days when the roles will be reversed. Having a training partner also makes some exercises and work outs easier or safer to do such as long-distance runs, bicycle rides, or simply spotting for you on the bench press. Not wanting to let down a buddy, plus the natural competitiveness that results from two males pushing each other, makes having a training partner something to consider.

• Shower the same time you work out to save a bunch of get-ready time. If your usual routine is a morning shower, then maybe your work out should be in the morning too so that you only have to go through the clean-up routine one time per day.

• Take advantage of vacation days. Have a lot of them piled up? See if you can take off some half-days and spend the extra free time on your long run or bike ride, or a peaceful (but sweaty) couple of hours at the gym. If your company offers shorter summer hours

on Friday, use the extra time for a longer work out that day.

• Don't shop. Seriously, only go on shopping trips when you're specifically looking for something. Shopping has become entertainment in itself and nothing can eat up an afternoon quicker than wandering through the air-conditioned halls and food courts of a shopping mall.

• Join a sports league. Besides the cross-training aspect, being involved in a team sport where they absolutely expect you to show up, preferably in shape, can be a powerful motivator that forces you to schedule training time. Just make sure it's an active sport, such as volleyball, soccer, basketball, or a similar aerobic activity. Golf and bowling don't qualify, sorry.

• Don't wait until you "feel" like exercising. That's a truly lame excuse. Your work out plan is a promise to yourself. You don't break promises, do you?

• Sign up for a competitive event a month or so away. You've already set

goals in Chapter 3, "Questions to Ask Yourself," but this is different. It should be a competitive event such as a 5K, a bicycle race, or something similar that has nothing to do with racing a dirt bike. It gives you one more reason to stay focused on your training because none of us wants to look like a dork out there, especially in front of an audience. A lot of these non-motorcycling races offer such extras as T-shirts, food, and even post-race parties. Incentives are a nice reward for staying focused on your training.

• Walk the dog. If you don't have one, get one. Every guy needs a dog and a playful mutt will force you to spend more time outside, playing, and of course, going for walks. Both you and the dog will benefit.

• Injured so you can't lift weights or run? Then walk. Buy a pedometer, a device that keeps track of the number of steps you've taken, and aim for 10,000 steps per day.

• If your kids are involved in sports such as soccer or baseball, instead of passively watching them from the stands, use the time to walk around the perimeter of the playing field a few times. You'll still be able to cheer them on and watch the action, all while burning off calories.

• Switch gyms. Sometimes, it's where you're working out that provides the best excuse. Many people sign up at a gym, only to find out the place isn't quite right for them. Like bars and restaurants, different health clubs attract different crowds. If your main focus is weight training, but the club is heavily into aerobics classes for retirees, chances are you'll feel out of place and the weight room will be substandard. Or maybe your club is dominated by dudes with impossible muscles bulging in every direction who hog all the free weights so you can seldom get a hand on them. Another sign to look elsewhere.

• Don't expect miracles. Start slow and resist the typical American temptation to immediately go all-out. You want to be in this for the long haul. After the initial burst of enthusiasm and quick results, you hit a plateau and suddenly your work out is mostly work.

MUSIC MAKES YOU STRONGER

It's been proven time and again in studies that working out, especially when doing cardio work, seems easier when you've got your tunes playing in your ears. You pay more attention to the music and don't focus on the demands of your work out, meaning you're less likely to wimp out. Get one of the lightweight MP3 players that you can strap to your arm, and load it with your favorite road and work out music.

This is normal and to be expected, so accept it as what it is: reality. It took you years to get out of shape and you won't suddenly wake up one morning as a rippling muscled stud. It takes time and a lifetime commitment. Be a survivor, not a wimp. Never surrender. Most people drop their exercise program after no more than three months. Don't be one of them.

Avoiding Burnout

There are damn few things you can do in life repeatedly, day after day and month after month, without eventually getting burned out. That's why vacations were invented.

Training is the same way. If you get too bored with your work out, you might quit it altogether. It's better to give yourself periodic mental and physical vacations, so you can come back to your work out plan with a fresh perspective. Often, you'll come back from a few days of doing nothing, to seeing some big improvements because you're fresh and rested.

Your muscles get bored too and you may stop seeing improvements. If you do the same activities week in and week out, your body adapts to the stress and puts you smack dab on top of a plateau. The exercises simply aren't as challenging, and while you won't see a loss of fitness, you won't see any gains either. You're in a rut, which leads to discouragement, boredom, and suddenly you're not working out at all anymore. It goes from being the part of the day you looked forward to, to just another chore on the long list.

Your body and mind need change in order to constantly boost their performance and stay fresh. Do some cross-training work outs or sports and change your work out routine in small ways. Try some new exercises; if you've been running a lot, switch to a bicycle for your aerobic work and vice versa. Mix in other activities like swimming or experiment with some of the gym's other equipment that you've been avoiding. Hire a personal trainer for one session to give you an objective view of your condition and training. Try a different gym or work out at a different time of day; take that Tae Bo kickboxing or stationary bike "spinning" class the spandex crowd is doing. The goal is the same: Lift yourself out of the rut and put some new stresses on your body so it keeps improving. That's the best way to avoid exercise burnout and the need to come up with excuses why you can't do anything on that day.

One more thing: To get the best results, do the exercises that are hardest for you, not the easiest. We're typical

Your daily commute may actually be a work out in disguise. Try walking, bicycling, even running to work or school instead of driving or taking the bus. In grid-locked metro areas, bicyclists can usually beat the four-wheeled-commute even over relatively long distances. Carry a change of clothes and marvel at how much money you're saving while also getting into better shape.

Work out at lunch time. Run or walk or join a health club near your office. While your co-workers are overloading on calories, you're burning them.

If you're one of those people who look to the weather to decide whether or not you're going to work out, well, unless you live in San Diego, you can probably always find an excuse. One word of advice: Don't. Weather should not dictate your work out schedule.

I grew up in Wisconsin where snow and winter are just part of reality. Then I moved to Minnesota and found out what winter can really be like! While the summers are wonderful, the winters can be a challenge. Imagine sub-zero windchills, heavy snow, ice everywhere, and air so cold that it feels like you could cut it into bite-size pieces. But Minnesota also taught me something about training: Weather alone won't keep you from training if you're stubborn and determined. Since I'm both, I lost very few days to weather excuses. I was also surprised how much company I had outdoors on even the worst days. Other runners and cross-country skiers were everywhere. It's part attitude, part inner gut-check, and part simply knowing how to dress for the elements. With enough and the correct layers of wicking performance fabrics and head/ears/hand protection, even sub-zero days were still work out days. Snow? Heck, running through a few inches of the white stuff is like running on a beach. The resistance gives you stronger ankles.

My point is that weather really doesn't matter. It can add something special and beneficial to your work outs, rather than being a reason to cancel them completely. Bad weather is also a

lazy humans, so even in a work out program we naturally tend to spend most of our time doing the stuff that comes with the least effort.

What's the Weather?

Unless your training plan is all indoors, sooner or later you have to be outside if you want to put in those cardio miles. When it comes to exercising outdoors, a lot of people wimp out. They find an excuse to not run or bike because it's too hot, too cold, too wet, too windy, or too something. They're waiting for the mythical perfect weather day, meanwhile making excuses to skip their endurance training.

Now as long as you replace the outdoor training with comparable work on a stationary bicycle, elliptical trainer, or treadmill, that's okay. You're going to miss the special joys of being outside, the variety of terrain, the smells of fresh-cut grass, the people out walking the dog or working on their lawns, but that's your choice.

ENOUGH CLOTHES?

Here's a rule of thumb for being able to tell if you have the right mix of clothing layers on for a cold weather work out or at the starting line of your race: If you're warm and comfy while just standing around, you're overdressed. Shed some layers. Once you get moving or the gate drops, your muscles will generate all the heat you need. Also, avoid anything that's cotton for your work out. Wear the moisture-wicking technical clothing that allows your sweat to evaporate quickly. Cotton soaks up the sweat, gets cold, and then makes you colder still.

great time to have a work out partner. The other person will drag you outside and refuse to listen to your whiny excuses. Most likely, the next day you'll be the one dragging him out the door.

You should skip an outdoor work out under extreme circumstances like heavy thunderstorms with lightning, total whiteouts, and other truly dangerous conditions. But in most cases, suck it up and head out that door. You'll actually be glad you did.

TWO-MINUTE BOARD

- Not enough time is everyone's excuse, yet you always seem to find time for the things you really want to do. Well, you need to really want to get your work outs done.
- You don't find time, you manufacture it by putting it in your daily schedule as an appointment with yourself.
- Train while doing something else. Work out in front of the TV.
- Don't go looking for excuses to skip your work out, look for ways to make sure you do it.
- If you're pressed for time, simplify your work out and make it more intense. You'll still get 90 percent of the benefits.
- Think of the whole world as your work out area. It's not just about getting to the gym by a certain time.
- Get a training partner. There will be days when your partner drags you to your work out and other days when you'll be dragging your partner along. But you'll both get your work outs done.

Join a sports league. You'll make the time for it and you'll get a work out. Just make sure it's a sport that provides a work out, not a game like bowling or golf. What you're looking for is an excuse is to sweat, use your muscles, and have some fun at the same time.

When you're at the health club, use your time working out, not socializing. You can always invite someone to join you at the juice bar or coffee shop later.

Chapter 9

TRAINING TOYS

Nothing builds strong wrists and forearms faster than a wristroller trainer. This is a commercial version, but you can build one for next to nothing from a piece of closet rod and four feet of rope. Hold the wristroller straight out with both arms and slowly wind the weight up, slowly unwind it back to the starting position. Your forearms will be burning in short order. Again, use your wrists only.

You've already learned about the basic equipment you need for your work out. In fact, you can get a tremendous work out with no equipment other than your body (see Chapter 3, "Core Strength"). Add to that the basics of a strength-building program based on free weights or machines, and you'd think that would pretty much cover things.

Not so. Take a walk through any sporting goods store and you'll see shelves full of devices promising all kinds of wonderful benefits. There are plenty of training toys out there and more are being created every day. Some really do deliver training benefits, while adding variety and fresh enthusiasm to your work outs. There are work out toys that will help improve your endurance, reflexes, grip, balance, and timing. Most of them are inexpensive enough to be worth a try. Some are simply so fun or easy to use that you can do the exercises while doing something else—driving, watching TV, or working at the office.

Keep in mind that only a couple of these items are must-haves; the rest are simply fun additions to your work out toy collection.

Since finding some of these products can be a hassle, your best bet is to go online unless you've got a really well-equipped sporting goods store nearby. Things like hand grippers are easy to find, but medicine balls, balance boards, and even a wide selection of heart rate monitors can be tough to locate. Finally, there's a good reason to go shopping.

Heart Rate Monitors
How hard are you really working? It's probably not nearly as hard as you think. The best way to accurately answer this question is by using a heart

rate monitor (HRM). For endurance training that delivers the goods, a heart rate monitor is well worth the price—about $80 for the base models. The monitor allows you to train at your body's estimated target zone, a percentage of your maximum heart rate zone (HRMax). You determine your HRMax by subtracting your age from 220. If you're 30 years old, your maximum heart rate would be 190. Your maximum heart rate is a general measure of your cardiovascular fitness.

For maximum aerobic training results, you need to train at 70 to 80 percent of your HRMax for 40 to 60 minutes per day, and preferably three to four times a week. Using the example of a 30-year-old's HRMax numbers of 190, that means training at a pace where the heart rate is in the 130 to 150 zone (70 to 80 percent of 190). You train most efficiently and see the greatest endurance-building results when you keep your heart rate within this target zone.

If weight loss is your focus, then training at 60 to 70 percent of your HRMax (114 to 130, using the example above) is recommended. Again, this has to be for at least 40 minutes and three to four times a week.

A heart rate monitor is nothing more than an electronic nag that will remind you to train at a level where you'll get the most benefit. It keeps you honest by telling you whether or not you're really working hard enough.

However, the whole HRMax formula has a built-in flaw. Because it's an average, the HRMax formula was never intended to provide an absolute number for elite athletes or people who regularly exercise at a high level. If you're already in very good shape, your target heart rate zone may be anywhere from 20 to 30 points lower than what the formula says. Short of doing exhaustive tests, there's no easy way to establish what a very fit person's HRMax really is. If you fall into this category, then you're

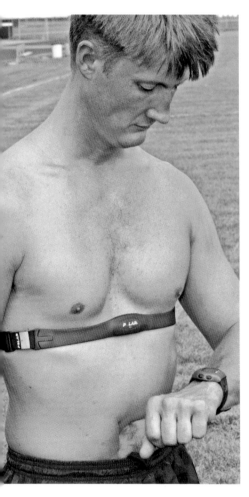

A heart rate monitor (HRM) consists of a transmitter that you wear around your chest and a receiver that doubles as a running watch. An HRM allows you to keep track of your heart rate and tells you how hard you're really working. The goal is to stay within the range that produces the best results, whether it's endurance or weight loss.

YESTERDAY'S NEWS

Take a half dozen sheets of yesterday's newspaper and open them up on a table or your desk at work. Using only one hand, start from the center and slowly crumble the sheet of newspaper into a tight little ball. Then switch hands. Crumble three or four pages per hand per day, and you'll have mitts of steel.

Here's a no-cost way to build a stronger grip. Open up a newspaper flat on a table. Starting from the center of the page, slowly crunch the paper up into a ball using your fingers. Do five pages with each hand and you'll know you did some serious work.

DUCT TAPE

For a stronger grip, here's a tip if you have your own set of free weight equipment. Wrap a couple of layers of duct tape around the bar or dumbbell, where your hands go. Periodically—every month or so—add another layer or two of duct tape. By increasing the diameter of the bars, you're forcing your hands to adjust and build more muscle for a better hold on the bar as you do your exercises.

There are various medicine ball exercises, but the basics involve twisting, throwing, and catching in a continuous smooth motion. This works your abdominals and arms. Training with a medicine ball is almost like playing, rather than working out, but the benefits are real.

probably also pretty much in touch with what your body can and can't do. You know from experience when you're really working at a high level of effort. For this reason, heart rate monitors are best for people at the beginning and intermediate stages of aerobic fitness. Elite athletes rely on them more to fine-tune and build up to a peak level in preparation for a specific race than as a cardio training nag.

Heart rate monitors consist of an elastic chest strap containing the wireless transmitter, and a monitor that doubles as a running watch and a receiver for the information from the transmitter. There aren't any wires and you'll hardly notice you have it on.

Do you need one? Yes and no. You can certainly run, bike, and cross-country ski without one and they're not cheap. Plus, as I've explained, if you're already extremely fit the standard formula for calculating your HRMax doesn't apply. So, if you're a stubborn SOB who's good at pushing yourself along at a brisk pace, you can do without a heart rate monitor. If, however, you need a nudge and some nagging to remind you to work as hard as you should be working, a heart rate monitor will help you do so.

One great use for a heart rate monitor is while practicing on your MX bike. Just as with going running, the monitor can remind you to dig down and push your body at a harder pace or ride more laps. You can usually mount the watch receiver to the handlebar pad and the transmitter strap fits easily under your riding jersey.

Polar is the premier brand name in heart rate monitors, but you can also find versions made by Nike and Oregon

Scientific, among others. Some models include a GPS function to provide you not only with a report on how fast your heart is ticking over, but also exact distance covered during a work out. As usual, the more bells and whistles offered, the more you'll pay for the privilege of using it. Top of the line models will cost $200 plus.

Medicine Balls

Medicine balls are seriously old school. Your grandfather was using one in gym class back in the dark ages. Medicine balls have come back into fashion for a good reason: They work. Medicine balls build core trunk strength and joint integrity. These benefits are important because no matter how strong your muscles are, you're really only as strong as your joints allow you to be. Joints are the weak link in the muscular chain. Medicine balls effectively work joints due to the range of motion used in throwing and catching the ball, which adds strength and flexibility. In addition, explosive high-powered movements are best learned by training in an explosive manner, and medicine balls provide exactly that type of quick-reaction exercise.

If you doubt any of this, just consider that most NBA and NFL teams have their players do a variety of medicine ball exercises to develop explosive strength. Track athletes use them to develop speed, and, of course, boxers have used them for decades to become rock hard and able to absorb punches.

So what will a medicine ball do for a motocross rider? When you think about what your muscles are doing while riding—controlling and balancing

a top-heavy object that wants to head off in all different directions—with throwing and catching a heavy medicine ball, you can appreciate the similarities. Picking up, rotating, and throwing or catching a medicine ball makes your upper body rotate. Unleash the power to throw the ball toward the wall or a training partner, then rotate and absorb the energy of catching the ball. A 10-pound medicine ball thrown though the air contains a lot of energy that your muscles have to quickly get under control. It's a great total body work out that builds a stronger trunk, rotator cuff, back, abs, and hip muscles.

There are two types of medicine balls, the kind that bounce and the kind that don't. If you're going to be working out alone, the bouncy type offers the greatest number of exercise opportunities because you can throw and rebound the ball against a masonry wall. The bouncing type cost more than the no-bounce versions. Weights vary from 1 kilogram (about 2 pounds) to 8 or 10 kilograms (about 16 to 20 pounds). The size you'll need will be someplace in the middle such as a 4 kilogram (about 9 pounds). Don't go nuts on weight; it's the action and velocity, rather than the sheer weight of the ball, that provides the training benefits. If it's too heavy, you won't be able to throw it very hard or far. Besides being a great overall work out, throwing a medicine ball is also one of those fun exercises that you don't mind doing.

Some medicine balls come with a built-in handle. These have become popular as an alternative to dumbbells while doing various exercises. They provide an easy way to add weight when doing crunches, sit-ups, and similar core routines.

Medicine balls vary in price by weight, material, and whether they bounce or not. For a 4-kilogram bouncing version, expect to pay about $40. A no-bounce will usually be about $10 cheaper. Shop around and try to find one locally because the shipping charges for a heavier ball can be quite expensive.

Chin-Up/Pull-Up Bar

Most gyms don't offer these anymore (if they ever did in the first place) so go buy one. Get the kind that has brackets you can screw into the door jam, rather than ones that use adjustable tension. A chin-up bar works your whole upper body, builds strength fast because it's a tough exercise, and most cost $20 or less. Get one and install it someplace where you have to walk under it regularly as a reminder to stop and spend a minute or two building your arms and shoulders each day.

Every racer should have a chin-up bar someplace in his house where he'll pass by it frequently. Use it every chance you get and you'll have shoulders like the Rocky Mountains. Buy the kind that screws in place into the doorway.

Every racer should have a chin-up bar at home and should be using it daily. Start with chin-ups (palms facing you) and graduate to pull-ups (palms facing away). See Chapter 3 for details and additional exercise variations. Nothing else builds stronger shoulders, backs, and arms as quickly.

Balance Boards

Humans take for granted the sheer difficulty and complex physiology that allows us to walk upright. It's a difficult balancing trick that virtually no other animal has mastered. Of course, as motorcycle riders, balance is something we absolutely require unless we want to earn the nickname Crash.

Training your muscles to instantly react to an unstable situation is the role of balance or "wobble" boards. These are typically 15- to 20-inch-diameter disks with varying or adjustable wobble angles available. They're useful for

Motorcycles are all about balance and one way to improve yours is to use a balance or wobble board. Ski racers have used them for years in their training because it works both your balance and your reflexes at the same time.

ONLINE GEAR SOURCES

The following retailers have online stores that carry the products listed above as well as other exercise gear. Boot up the computer and surf over to:

Amazon.com: Stocks a wide variety of exercise gear from a number of sources. Maybe not the first place you'd think to look, but definitely check it out.

Bodytrends.com: All types of fitness, aerobic, and weight-loss products

Exertools.com: Gym balls, medicine balls, wobble boards, and more.

Fitbuy.com: A broad selection of products; good prices and fast shipping. Definitely worth a visit

Fitter1.com: Canadian fitness company that sells a wide variety of training gear. Great selection

JumpUSA.com: Lots of medicine balls and lots of other products. The website also provides very good training information to help you make purchasing decisions

Karatedepot.com: Martial arts, strength, and flexibility training aids

Muscledriver.com: Primarily strength-training gear

REI.com: A member coop rather than a commercial chain, REI specializes in outdoor gear. Strictly the best stuff and a favorite source of gear for rock climbers, campers, skiers, and other outdoor sports enthusiasts. Look for items like Power Putty and other training gear

Roadrunnersports.com: The premier online source for running shoes and gear. Provides online shoe-buying advice that will help you get the right pair of real running shoes

home to over two dozen bones, an equal number of ligaments and joints, and all of it is balled up into a fist-sized space. There's not much room for muscle in there.

If you've ever watched the classic motorcycle racing movie, "On Any Sunday," you probably remember seeing flat track star Mert Lawwill driving to a race and working a spring-type hand gripper for what seemed like the whole trip. Grippers are about as low-tech as they come, but they should still be an essential part of your work out gear. Buy several and sprinkle them around your house, truck, and office so they're always available. Work them while watching TV, during your commute, sitting in meetings, riding the school bus, and so on. Your connection to that dirt bike is through your hands and forearms, and a strong grip is an essential element if you want to stay in control.

Want a tougher work out? Instead of squeezing the hand gripper open and shut, try to hold it completely shut for one minute. If you can do this easily,

improving your balance, overall agility, and reaction time, plus they work the small muscles that most other work outs ignore. They cost from $30 to $80 and the ones made out of wood are more rigid (good), while the plastic ones are sometimes too flexible (bad). One version, the Reebok Core Board, responds to movement by pushing back against your reaction adding a three-dimensional aspect to the exercise.

You can use balance boards in the same way as stability balls, for exercises such as push-ups. Or, if you've gotten good at standing on the balance board, increase the difficulty by holding or throwing a medicine ball! While definitely not an essential piece of work out gear, it provides some variety and new challenges for your muscles that you won't get anywhere else.

Hand Grippers

The human hand doesn't have much inherent strength. A man's hand is

Squeezing a hand gripper while on your commute or headed for the races is a time-honored way of building your grip. Want it tougher? Try to hold the gripper closed for one full minute—put a dollar bill between the grip handles to be sure it's really closed tight. If you can do this easily, you need a stiffer gripper.

then the gripper is too light-duty and you need to get something stiffer.

Push-Up Lifts

Push-up bars raise you a few inches further from the floor in order to make your push-ups more difficult. It sounds sadistic, but the payoff is a bigger, stronger chest and more strength because the muscles worked are the pectorals (chest) and triceps. The lift stands provide a greater range of motion for a more efficient work out. You can also use hexagonal dumbbells (the ones with the flat edges) for the same effect. Push-up lifts cost about $10 and most sporting goods stores stock them.

Ab Rollers

Used for physical training (PT) in the military for years, this is just a set of wheels with a pipe running through it. In use, you start on your knees with the ab roller pipe grasped in front of you. Slowly roll forward, until—assuming you can—your body is stretched out and parallel to the floor. Then slowly roll it back and start over. The ab roller does a great job of stretching and toning your upper and lower abdominals and shoulders. This is definitely one exercise

Your work out toy box can easily hold these two. The plastic gray fist holds Power Putty, a thick blue gel that works your fingers in both directions and is a favorite of rock climbers for a steel-fingered grip that won't give up. The odd-looking Z-bar has knobs that bounce in unpredictable directions. A fun way to hone your reflexes to razor-edged sharpness.

you will feel the first time you do it, so take it easy. Since you can find ab rollers for around $10 in stores, they're a cheap and worthwhile addition to your work out toy box.

Power Putty

Most grip exercisers only work your hands in one direction with the closing motion. Power Putty works hands and fingers in both directions, which is why it's a long-time favorite of rock climbers and in rehab situations. Rock climbers need fingers of steel and can't afford a slip, which should be a good enough endorsement. Power Putty is a silicone rubber compound that comes in four degrees of firmness (difficulty), and either the Med/Firm or Hard will give your hands and fingers a serious work out. Power Putty comes in a fist-shaped plastic container that looks cool on your desk and costs about $12. Included in the package are instructions and 12 exercises.

Reaction Balls

Variously called Reaction Balls and Z-Balls, this is a knobby ball that bounces in unpredictable ways. There are seven knobs that send the ball careening off in every direction, but the knobs also keep it from bouncing in impossible-to-catch ways. Your job

The abs roller looks like a gimmick, but helps build your abdominals. You roll it slowly forward from a kneeling position and then roll it back. You'll definitely feel it working, so take it easy the first few times. To use, kneel on the floor and slowly roll forward until you feel it in your abdominals. Pause and roll back. This is a tough exercise, so go easy and don't strain.

is to snag it, and it's really not easy, to give your reflexes quite a work out. While catching it may not be easy, it's a lot of fun to try, especially with a training partner. It's one of those happily mindless exercises that can keep you occupied for hours.

The Z Ball costs about $11 and comes in a variety of colors. You'll probably have to order online to get one, although some tennis shops will have them in stock.

The Gripp

Considering my height and weight, I have relatively short fingers (genetics at work), so I need all the strength I can pack into these stubby nubs. While it doesn't look like much, The Gripp works your fingers, hands, wrists, and forearms in ways you'll definitely feel. The Gripp is simple to carry around or have at hand on your desk, and at $10 it's another inexpensive work out toy. Just squeeze and release repeatedly. You gain strength, endurance, and a better feel for the controls.

Heavy Bag

There's something very male and elemental in punching a heavy bag. It's also a helluva work out for your shoulders and arms, and it improves your timing. A great stress reliever, too. A heavy bag will cost from $60 to $100 and I personally prefer the ones intended for martial arts rather than boxing because the martial arts version can also be used for kicks. You may need gloves at first (perhaps a pair of old MX gloves) because your knuckles will take a beating.

By the way, throwing a punch is something every guy thinks he knows how to do, and very few actually do. It's a complex motion that actually comes from your hips, not your shoulders. Your wrist must be straight when it contacts the bag, not crooked. Do it wrong, and you can sprain your wrists big-time. To learn how to properly throw a punch, sign up for a martial arts class. Most offer a low-cost introductory program and they'll teach you how to actually throw a strong punch, not those limp-wrist girly love taps.

TWO-MINUTE BOARD

- A heart rate monitor lets you know how hard you're working and whether you're in the optimal range for maximum training results.
- Medicine balls provide a tough and comprehensive work out for muscles, joints, and your reflexes that most people find fun to do. And anything that's fun, you'll do more often.
- A chin-up bar in your house really isn't optional. You flat out need one.
- There are a lot of training toys that can build a stronger vise-like grip and, since most of them are small, you should have one with you during your daily commute.
- Find ways to make push-ups tougher. Push-up lifts are one easy to use training toy that increases the benefits from your push-ups.

Chapter 10

RACE WEEKEND

So you've done your training; you're feeling good about yourself and your conditioning. Now, there's a race weekend looming and you need to prepare for it. The preparation includes what you bring along, how you warm up, how you approach practice, and how you spend your time while waiting for your race to start.

Foods that Make You Fast

If you've gotten serious about your training—and why else would you be reading this book—you've probably cleaned up your diet by eliminating a lot of fatty, salty, non-nutritious junk that does nothing except slow you down, lard you up, and lay down a foundation for future health problems. That's been the advice throughout this book and you're not going to find a trainer in any sport who thinks otherwise.

Then ask yourself why you would mess everything up by adding chips, pop, and other high-calorie crap to your take-to-the-races goodies bag? If a food is bad for you during the week, it doesn't magically become beneficial on weekends. In fact, race day is when proper energy intake is most crucial. You've been investing all those hours in training and eating right so you can be at your best on a race weekend with your body performing at its maximum potential. Race day is the wrong day to fall off the healthy foods wagon.

Are you one of those riders who skips eating on race day because you worry about losing your lunch due to nerves or over-exertion? Or are you one of the guys in line at the concession stand for a chili dog with all the fixings

This is your body's race-day fuel. What you eat in the morning is going to affect your energy level for the entire day. Make race-day breakfast healthy with a lot of complex carbs. Whole-grain cereal, fresh fruit, and a whole-grain bagel are quick, simple, and easy to bring along. On the road early? Just put the cereal in a bag and add milk. Donuts are nothing but fat and sugar and will slow you down.

KEEPING YOUR COOL

No matter what kind of shape you're in, it won't make a difference if heat and dehydration suck all that energy out of you. Some tips on keeping your race day cool:

• Wear vented gear. This is a no-brainer. Moose Racing's Sahara line and the AC gear from Thor are personal favorites when I want a breeze blowing over my bod.

• Take advantage of shade, both where you park in the pits and while waiting for your race to stage. If you don't have a pop-up canopy of some kind, get one—another no-brainer.

• Bring a water bottle to the line and drink just before your moto. Use some of it or a second bottle to pour over your jersey just before the start.

• Soak your jersey in water before heading for the start line. The evaporation will cool you off just like air conditioning.

• Find someone to hold an umbrella over your head to give you some shade on exposed start lines.

• Keep your helmet off until the last couple of minutes. Your head is a radiator, a major part of your body's cooling system. It needs airflow to throw off excess heat. Instead of buying the cheapest helmet out there, look for a helmet that has lots of venting and is as lightweight as possible while still meeting safety standards.

• On the hottest days, consider wearing a CamelBack even for motocross.

• A wet, cold towel draped around your neck will cool your body quickly. It's great before a moto and heaven afterward.

• Be aware of heat-related warning signs: Red, hot, sweaty skin—or no sweat at all—cramps, headache, lightheadedness, and fatigue will occur long before heat stroke. Get out of the heat and seek medical attention.

Cool it! On a really hot day, find ways to cool off between motos. If you're really hot and can't seem to get cool, have someone hose you down. Soak a towel in the cold water in the bottom of your cooler and drape the towel around your neck and shoulders, cooling off the big arteries carrying blood to your brain.

Race-day morning is a busy time, but don't use that as an excuse to chow down on a fatty fast food breakfast or a box of glazed donuts. Fuel your body properly just as you'd do before any athletic event.

between motos? Neither approach is the right one.

You need food on race day because you're going to be burning lots of calories. Just as the bike needs fresh gas between motos, you need to refuel as well. What you need is food that's quickly and easily digested, with high water content and complex carbohydrates that deliver long-term energy. You want to eat on race day so you have energy left for those grueling second motos when your competitors are sucking wind and fading fast.

It's not just what's in your cooler, however. Your race day eating begins earlier.

Race Day Breakfast

Whether you're driving to the race or getting there the day before and overnighting, eat breakfast. Always eat breakfast, period. Your bike won't start with an empty gas tank and neither will you. By 6 a.m., your body has gone at least eight hours without any fuel being added to its tank. How do you expect to be at your physical best while sucking fumes?

By "eat breakfast," I don't mean doughnuts or sugary cereals that are all empty calories. If there's a cartoon character on the cereal box, it's junk food. Garbage in still equals garbage out.

Instead, your breakfast should be a healthy one with a selection of healthy foods that will get you quickly refueled and ready for the long day ahead. That means things like:

• Whole-grain cereal (lots of fiber, little sugar) with fresh berries, bananas, or oatmeal.
• Orange juice (the real stuff).
• Coffee (no cream, no sugar).
• Whole-wheat toast with jam (easy on the butter, or none at all).
• Blueberry pancakes.
• Scrambled eggs.

Avoid high-fat foods like:
• Bacon or breakfast sausages.
• Giant muffins (they're really cake by another name).
• Or any of the fast-food joint's "breakfast" sandwiches.

Mid-Day Fuel Stop

Race days can easily be 12 hours long, yet many riders skip eating for the duration. Usually it's because of concerns about having enough time between races, nervousness, or uncertainty about whether they even should eat.

The short answer is yes, you do need to eat something. Don't just eat a bag of chips or the concession stand hot dogs. You wouldn't dump a gallon of old varnished gas into your race bike, and you also shouldn't be dumping junk into your body. You want basic protein and complex carbs again, just as if you were doing a pre-work out lunch. You also need it to be simple, easy to fix, and easy to haul along because you've got enough to do and not a lot of time. The smart approach is to make your race-day lunch the day ahead, seal it in plastic, and throw it into your cooler so it's ready when you need it. Some suggestions:
• Turkey sandwich with tomato (mustard instead of mayo) or butter on the bread).
• Peanut butter and jelly sandwich.
• Any of the legitimate energy bars (PowerBar, Clif Bars, etc.).
• Grapes, apples, plums, pears, or other juicy fruits that are water-rich.

Don't try and go the whole race day without eating or you'll be sucking wind by the time the second moto rolls around. Instead of a chili dog from the concession stand, bring along foods that will deliver long-lasting energy. Bananas, apples, energy bars, and a peanut butter and jelly sandwich are all good and easy choices.

• Bananas, because they're as close to being the perfect endurance food as anything scientists have been able to come up with in their labs, but Mom Nature beat them to the punch. Bananas are loaded with potassium, which is rapidly depleted as you sweat.
• Wash down your lunch with plenty of water or a real energy drink, not one of the sugary concoctions that fill the grocery store shelves.
• If you can't or won't find time to eat a quick lunch, then go with the energy supplements that marathon runners and bicyclists use: energy gels and drinks. They won't fill you up, but they can supply a quick energy boost when you most need it. However, as with any

RACE IN THE HEAT? THEN TRAIN IN THE HEAT

Since you spend most of your racing time outside in the heat and humidity, your endurance training should be under the same conditions. You can be in awesome cardio condition from hours on the treadmill or exercise bike in the comfort of the air-conditioned health club, or from running in the evening when it's cooled off, but you'll wilt like a pansy on a humid summer day at the races. Try to do most of your endurance training under conditions that match what you'll encounter on race day.

training food, experiment with the product well before race day. Find out if you can stand the taste, which tends to be syrupy sweet and see if your stomach tolerates them.

Pack Your Cooler

Your cooler is second only to your toolbox in necessity. Besides holding your day's liquids and perhaps a post-race celebration beer, ice is a necessity for first aid. It comes in handy for bumps and bruises, or to cool you off quickly on very hot days.

Stock your cooler with:

• Bottles of water you can carry around.

• An insulated water jug filled with ice so that during the course of the day, instead of drinking pop, have some ice water. It's cheap or free, and much better for you.

• Two or three bottles of an electrolyte replacement sports drink; you want the stuff that's intended for distance runners, bicyclists, and other endurance athletes. Don't drink the glorified soft drinks that are so popular now; drink a full bottle between every one of your motos so you're properly hydrated.

• You might want to have a can or two of one of the energy drinks (Red Bull, etc.) in your cooler; the jury is out as to whether they really deliver a noticeable benefit, but if you like how they taste, you might find them useful. These drinks aren't intended to rehydrate you, but rather replace essential nutrients that are lost as you sweat.

Staying Hydrated

It seems like most race days are also days of weather extremes. Either it's hot and humid, or wet and hot, or wet and cold. Perfect weather seems to be the exception. Toss in that most race tracks are out in the open with little or no shade, and it's a hot, hot world we race in. With the heat and the level of physical exertion we put out, we lose a lot of water as we sweat. In fact, your late-day race fatigue may be due more to dehydration than to muscle fatigue.

Stay well hydrated, even on cool days when you think you're probably not sweating but you really are. Water lubes your muscles and keeps them from getting stiff, sore, and tired. The easy way to do this is to bring along a large insulated water container. Fill it with a bag of ice and fresh water and you're set for the day.

• Make a point of staying hydrated throughout the day. See "The Nixon Test" for how you know if your body has enough liquids in it. This means drinking a lot, pretty much continuously throughout the day. Your body doesn't give you a lot of advance warning that you need something to drink. Thirst is slow to make itself known. That's why the Nixon Test is a more reliable indicator.

• Sweat is the body's cooling system. As it evaporates off your skin, it cools you. But keep in mind that when the humidity is above 75 percent, the sweat never really evaporates and you never get cooler.

• How much do you sweat? Hard exercise—which is what racing a bike is—can mean your body will lose up to one-half gallon of water per hour. Hidden within all that sweat are the electrolytes (sodium and potassium) that are fundamental to keeping your muscles cranking along at full power. All that sweat pouring out of your body soon shows up as weight loss, fatigue, confusion, diminished reflexes, cramping muscles, and can ultimately result in unconsciousness or death. While that's unlikely for most motocross riders, off-road riders with their day-long stints in the saddle especially need to be concerned about staying hydrated.

WATER OR SPORTS DRINK?

What hydrates better and faster? Water or a sports drink? Assuming we're talking about a real sports drink, then the answer is the sports drink does. There are three reasons:

1. Fluids are absorbed through the gut and into the bloodstream when their *osmolality* closely matches that of your blood. Osmolality is the concentration of dissolved particles in a fluid, and sports drinks contain these (sodium, etc.), while water doesn't. So sports drinks hit your bloodstream quicker.

2. Sodium and other nutrients help regulate your body's fluid balance. Again, sports drinks have these nutrients and water doesn't.

3. The sodium in the sports drinks stimulates thirst, making you drink more. That's a good thing, because your body is slow to announce that it's thirsty.

Look for a sports drink that contains at least 15 miligrams of sodium per ounce (check the label). Some studies indicate that sports drinks with carbohydrates and protein are the most effective at being quickly absorbed by your body and put to use.

None of this means you shouldn't drink water. It's still vital for your body, less expensive, and more convenient to bring along. Oftentimes, it's all you really need.

By the way, this isn't just a summer-time problem. Don't think that just because it's cool that you're not sweating. You can sweat nearly as heavily on a cool or downright cold day as you can on the hottest summer day. It's sneakier water loss and it's complicated by the fact that you probably won't be drinking as much. Again, refer to The Nixon Test to see if you're drinking enough.

Nap Time and Other Tricks

Racing is stressful for both mind and body. One way to deal with the stress is to take a nap. If there's time between your motos, find a quiet comfortable spot and catch a quick snooze—just be sure someone will wake you in time for your race. Jeremy McGrath, among others, often takes a nap before his main events. You should too.

Besides giving your body a chance to spin down and recoup, a light nap of 15 or 20 minutes refreshes your mind. Racing isn't just physical. Your brain needs to be sharp and focused on the job.

For those of you who like coffee (the real stuff, with caffeine), it may boost your performance a notch or two. In many studies, endurance athletes shown enhanced resistance to fatigue if they drink a cup of coffee 20 to 30 minutes before a race.

A quick emergency pick-me-up can come from soft drinks—the full-on sugary stuff. Take the top off and let it defizz first. Besides the sugar hit, there's caffeine too. Marathon runners and bicyclists sometimes go with de-fizzed pop when they feel like they're suffering from low blood sugar (headache, muscle fatigue, dizziness).

Warming Up

With so much effort focused on keeping cool, you also need to think about warming up. Just as you'd do before a work out, you need to prepare your muscles for what's ahead.

The photos that follow show some suggested warm-ups, which should already be familiar to you. Additional things to remember:

• Warm-up and stretch before practice. Practice time is the most dangerous and often most physically demanding point of your race day. You're dealing with the idiots who have to "win" practice, a wet and muddy track, the new obstacles the owner's bulldozer has created, and other challenges. No need to add cold muscles that can easily be strained or torn to the list, so stretch first.

•Walk or bicycle to the riders' meeting, and around the track and pits.

THE NIXON TEST

Want to know if you're properly hydrated on a hot day? Conduct the Nixon Test. Huh, what? You're properly hydrated if your urine is "perfectly clear", a famous line from one of our 37th president's speeches. If it's not clear, knock back some more water or sports drink until it is.

Don't park yourself in a lawn chair between motos and veg. Move around and stay warmed up and loose. A good way to do this is to bicycle around the pits to study your racing lines and see how the track is changing. Bicycle to the riders' meeting.

A mountain bike should be standard training equipment for any dirt biker, but it's also good on race day as a way to keep your muscles warmed up and ready. Walking has the same benefits. Walk or bike around, watch some other motos, check the results from the first race, etc.

• Rest periodically and between motos, but don't park your butt in the lawn chair nonstop. Get up, walk around, and stay loose. Otherwise you end up with stiff, creaky muscles and get to spend the first lap waking your body up.

Six Quick Warm-Up Stretches

1. Bend your arms over your back. This stretch loosens up your back. Hold for a count of 20.

2. Windmill, both arms are in motion first in the same direction, and then in opposite directions at the same time.

3. Side stretch, standing upright, with arms to the side. Stretch as far as you can to the left and hold for a count of 20; then stretch to the right for another 20 count.

4. Groin stretch (one leg in front of the other, low to the ground). Hold for a count of 20, then take a giant step forward and repeat the 20 count.

5. Split or close to it. Do after the groin stretch. Your boots actually make this easier to do than you might think.

6. Do four or five quick push-ups to get your arms and shoulders loose and the blood flowing faster.

See Chapter 12 for forearm stretches to do while on the line that might prevent arm pump.

Stretch and warm up your muscles before you ride. The best time is just before your practice session, when your muscles are cold and stiff and most prone to injury. Be in your riding gear and hold each stretch for a count of 20. Kick it off with a behind the back forward stretch. With your arms behind you as shown, bend over as far as you can and hold the stretch.

Ever had a pulled groin muscle? You don't want one. So, drop into the lunge position shown by taking one big step forward, and hold the stretch for a count of 20. Then immediately take another big step forward to stretch the other side.

Go from the groin stretch to doing a split. Your boots actually make this easy to do because they anchor your legs in place. Go as low as you can with your legs as far apart as is comfortable. As with any stretch, you want to feel the muscles under tension, but not to the point of pain.

Finally, do four or five pushups to get your arms and shoulders limber. This may also help prevent arm pump.

Keep your cool before your moto. As the temperature goes up, your strength and endurance go down. If it's 80 degrees outside, your muscle strength is down about 20 percent. While other riders wait in the hot sun, find yourself some shade. Or have a buddy or family member hold an umbrella.

TWO-MINUTE BOARD

- Start your race day the same way you start every day: with a good healthy breakfast. Your body needs the right fuel to do its job.
- Avoid the track concession stand in favor of quality food you bring along. Whole-grain bagels, turkey sandwich, bananas, apples, and even a peanut butter and jelly sandwich.
- Sports drinks designed for endurance athletes hydrate you better and quicker than just water alone.
- Stay hydrated and stay cool. Drink a lot and stay in the shade as much as possible on really hot days, because you lose about 1 percent of your muscle strength for every degree above 65 degrees.
- Stretch and warm-up before riding, especially before the first practice session.
- Since you race in the heat, do your training in the heat. Your body needs to acclimate.

Chapter 11

BECOMING MORE FLUID AND FLEXIBLE

Flexibility isn't something we spend a lot of time thinking about. If we even waste a second or two considering it, it's usually an acknowledgement that we're either flexible or we're not, one of those god-given acts of nature like having blue eyes instead of brown.

If you watch the top riders at speed, you've probably noticed how they move fluidly around the bike and can dance this way and that on the pegs. There isn't any stiffness. They're very flexible. You can be too.

Flexibility is a joint's ability to move through a full range of motion. It can be improved with work, sometimes significantly. Here are the benefits of becoming more flexible:

• Improved physical performance; a flexible joint can move through a greater range of motion and requires less energy to do so. You work less while achieving more.

• Less chance of injury; flexible muscles stretch easily, rather than resisting to the point of tearing apart.

• Reduced muscle soreness.

• Increased blood flow to tissues, making them more elastic and better able to handle the stress of high performance sports.

• Less lower back pain (and your back takes a beating while racing).

• Improved muscle coordination so you react quicker.

• You feel stronger, with quicker reflexes. Working out or playing sports feels more natural and easier to do.

• Flexible muscles simply perform better than tight ones.

Isn't this Just Stretching?

If you're in the habit of stretching before a work out, you might consider that to be enough flexibility training, but you'd be wrong. Pre-work out stretching is usually too short in duration and focused on too few muscles.

That said, flexibility and what you might think of as stretching are intertwined. You use what are basically muscle-stretching routines to move a joint to its limits. Stretching the muscle is what eventually makes it more elastic.

Also, flexibility is "joint specific." Just because you can easily touch your toes, doesn't mean you're especially flexible. The person who can easily flop down and touch their toes may not be able to do something like reach around and scratch the small of their back. Identify the joints where you're

Bent Over

Put your hands behind your back and bend from the waist. Hold for a count of 20.

Torso Stretch

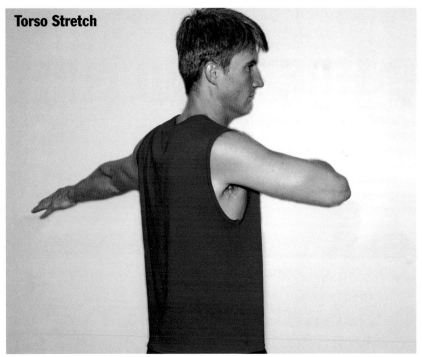

With arms out, twist all the way to one side and then twist all the way back. Do this five to ten times in quick succession.

Shoulder Stretch

Put one arm behind your back and neck as shown and use the other to apply pressure to the elbow to stretch it. Hold for a count of 20, then switch arms. This is really good for tight shoulders.

especially tight and inflexible, and then focus on those.

Another thing you need to understand about flexibility is that it comes in two flavors: static and dynamic. *Static flexibility* is your maximum range of motion without regard to speed of movement—it's a slow, easy stretch. *Dynamic flexibility* is the maximum range of motion at high speed—the force and velocity of sports in other words. You can have great static flexibility and be as limp as a shoelace, but still not have dynamic flexibility that will help you in sports. Obviously, you want the spring-steel qualities of dynamic flexibility for motocross.

Flexibility Exercise Rules

Like most things in life, there's a right way and a wrong way to do flexibility exercises. Here's the correct approach:

• Never stretch so far that you feel actual pain.
• Don't bounce or jerk. Smooth and slow is the rule.
• Flexibility takes time to acquire and progress can be very slow. Don't rush it or expect overnight miracle improvements.
• Breathe steadily, don't hold your breath.

• Hold a stretch for at least 20 seconds to no longer than a minute, release, and then repeat.
• Do these exercises while doing something else, like watching TV. You'll be more likely to actually do them and you'll get some use out of the otherwise wasted time.

Flex Exercises

These exercises will make you more flexible and able to respond quickly when the bike decides to zig while you were thinking zag. To have any effect, these exercises need to be done on a regular basis just like any other work out routine. The improvements will also take time to become noticeable. That's why I think the best time to do them is toward the end of your busy day with the TV blaring a mindless laugh track in the background. Do these flexibility work outs, and you'll use up a pleasant chunk of the typical TV show's 30 minutes. Alternately, use these flexibility exercises as a warm-up before doing your endurance or strength training program.

Lower Back

• Lie on your back and pull your right leg toward your chest. Keep your head

Arm/Shoulder

Stretch one arm across your chest and use the other arm to put it under tension. Hold for a count of 20, then switch arms.

Leg Stretch

With one hand supporting you against a wall, raise one leg and stretch it with your arm, as shown. Hold for a count of 20, then switch legs.

Groin Stretch

Take a long step forward and hold it—your basic lunge. Hold for a count of five, return to the start position, and lunge forward with the other leg. Do a set of 5 to 10 of these.

One-Legged Stretch

on the floor and your lower back flat. Hold for 30 seconds, and then do the other leg. Repeat three times for each leg.

• Stand with your feet slightly more than shoulder-width apart. Twist and lower your body down to touch

If the previous stretch is too easy, make it a lot tougher and also develop your balance with this stretch. Start with one leg held up against your buttocks as shown, then slowly bend over and touch the floor and then return to upright. Switch legs.

and hold one foot. You bend from the hips, not from the waist, to do this. Hold each stretch for 20 seconds, alternating between each leg. Do three sets and absolutely resist the temptation to bounce.

Hip and Groin

• Sit on the floor with your thighs parallel to the floor and your feet together, as shown. Lean forward slightly and apply pressure to your thighs with your forearms. Hold for 30 seconds. Repeat twice.

• Take a long step forward, as shown, lowering your back leg until it's almost touching the floor. Hold for 30 seconds and repeat with the other leg. Repeat twice for both legs.

Knee and Quads

• Using a wall for support, hold the top of one foot and gently pull the heel toward your buttocks. Hold for 30 seconds, then repeat with the other leg. Repeat twice.

• As with the previous exercise, hold the top of one foot and gently pull the heel toward your butt. However, when it

109

Butterfly Stretch

Sitting on the floor, bring your heels together in front of you and hold them as shown. Your forearms should rest on your thighs, pressing down on them. Bend your upper body forward to apply more pressure to your forearms and legs. Hold for a count of 20.

both arms and touch the floor between your legs. Hold for 20 seconds. Repeat the three stretches one more time.

• Do an Eagle. Lie on your back with arms out. Touch your right foot to your left hand while keeping your leg straight. Return to the starting position and switch legs. Repeat 3-5 times.

Other Ways to Become More Slinky-Like

The flexibility work out described here will make you much more flexible than you've probably ever been before. However, it's just a starting point. For increased flexibility plus a cross-training work out that supplements your other training, consider finding classes or a school in one of these disciplines:

Yoga: Yoga has gone mainstream and become part of the health club scene. Practicing yoga entails moving through a range of poses that not only increase flexibility but also build strength (not a lot), balance, speed, and (maybe) endurance. Look for a yoga class that advertises "power yoga" or *ashtanga* so you get the maximum work out benefit.

gets there, slowly bend from the waist and touch the floor (yes, this is tougher than it looks). Repeat with the other leg.

Shoulders

• Standing, hold the elbow of one arm with the hand of another and stretch it behind your back as shown. Hold for 15 seconds. Repeat twice for each arm.

• Standing, extend one arm across your chest and use your other arm to pin and stretch your arm. Hold for 15 seconds and repeat twice for each arm.

Hamstrings and Groin

• Be a butterfly (see photo above).

• Sit down and spread your legs in a "V" with your legs flat on the floor and your toes pointing up. Lean forward, and reach for or grasp one foot. Hold for 20 seconds. Repeat on the other leg, and then lean forward with

Eagle Stretch

This is a more advanced stretch, so you'll probably have to work up to it. Lying on the floor, legs outstretched, bring one leg all the way over your body so it's at a right angle to your torso. Touch your toes with the opposite arm, as shown. Hold for a count of 20. You are rotating from your hips and should have one or both shoulders on the floor.

considered a martial art, but there's nothing very martial about it. Balance, breathing, and flexibility are what you can expect to take away from this discipline.

None of the exercises in yoga, karate, or tai chi can be learned from a book or video. You absolutely need to sign up for classes taught by people who know what they're doing. Many schools will offer some kind of low-cost or free introductory period. Visit and watch a class before making any financial commitment or signing up. See if the classes offer the kind of work out and training you think would benefit your racing. Talk to other students before or after class, not just the instructor, to get a better feel for the program or school.

By the way, if you think racing a motorcycle is a test of nerves, believe me when I say there's nothing more intimidating than stepping onto a karate school floor for the very first time wearing a brand-new white belt. If you can gut your way through that, diving into a first turn with 40 other moto maniacs is relaxing by comparison.

If you want to become more flexible—and you should—then sign up at a martial arts school. Karate and similar martial arts will make you much more flexible, while also improving your timing, strength, self-confidence, balance, and reflexes. Since the classes are typically held in the evening, it's an easy way to add a workout to your schedule. *iStock.com*

Karate: Martial arts schools are traditionally very focused on developing flexibility and strength in order to be able to do the movements required by the discipline. Besides making you more flexible, expect improvements to your core strength, reflexes, and balance. Note that there are many variations of karate and other martial arts. While self-defense is the basis of all types of karate, look for schools that advertise their focus as being karate-*do* (literally, "the way of karate") instead of karate-*jutsu* (fighting techniques only).

Tai Chi: This is a kind of slow-motion calisthenics in which you're supposed to be very aware of your body and its movements. It's sometimes

TWO-MINUTE BOARD

- Flexibility allows you to react quicker to what the bike is doing. Being flexible may also prevent injuries and sprains.
- Too stiff? Flexibility is something you can teach your muscles by repeating exercises, just like making them stronger by pumping iron.
- Becoming more flexible will reduce lower back pain, improve muscle coordination, and make you feel stronger because you can react quicker.
- To both become more flexible and fine-tune your reflexes while getting a helluva work out, consider signing up for lessons at a local martial arts school.

Chapter 12

THEM'S THE BREAKS: INJURIES

It's called a risk sport for a reason. There's a few thousand different and totally thrilling ways to get hurt while racing. It's an old cliché, but there are only two kinds of dirt bikers: those who just crashed and those who are about to crash. Everybody crashes, from the rankest novice to the top pros—it comes with the territory. If the idea of getting body-slammed into the turf now and then bothers you, switch sports. Miniature golf sounds like more your style.

While crashing always sucks and usually hurts, if you're wearing decent riding gear, the crash will only occasionally cause serious injury. For a variety of reasons, the better shape you're in, the less you'll crash, and the odds of getting hurt when you do auger in go way, way down. Those are two more reasons to get into shape, just in case you're counting.

Still, sooner or later, every one of us is going to have one of those race days where we get to know the medics on a first-name basis. When it happens, physical training enters a new dimension. You're now faced with the challenge of staying in shape while recovering from an injury—two agendas that are mutually exclusive.

If your doctor insists that your daily exertion level should not exceed what's necessary to change channels with the remote, you might want to get a second opinion. There's a growing opinion in the medical field that "active healing," in which you follow an exercise plan right from the beginning rather than sitting around, leads to quicker recovery with fewer problems. Time spent in casts and slings is minimized in order to allow joints and muscles to regain flexibility quicker than if they were immobilized under a layer of plaster for a month.

Fair Warning
Before you read any further, keep this in mind: I'm not a doctor. I don't pretend to be a medical doctor or intend to become one. You should *not* choose to follow my advice about an injury over that of your personal physician. While this chapter was reviewed for accuracy by both a board-certified orthopedic surgeon who deals with many sports injuries (mine and others) and a paramedic with nearly 20 years of experience with motocross-related injuries, this chapter is in no way a substitute for seeing your own doctor in person. Racing injuries are complex, often with hidden internal injuries that won't be immediately obvious. There's simply no way a

A trip over the handlebars is never anybody's desired destination, but eventually it happens to everybody. This is why smart riders dress for the crash with good riding gear. All the protective gear you can buy is still cheaper than one trip to the ER.

book of this nature can offer more than a general discussion of the topic.

The bottom line is this: When in doubt about any type of injury, even one your racing buddies may think is no big deal, seek medical attention. Just having the track-side EMTs take a look

at you isn't the same as having a doctor do a complete exam. The EMTs and paramedics are good at what they do, but their job is only to stabilize and transport medical emergencies—get you to a hospital alive in other words, so a doctor can take over.

By the way, trackside first-aid providers aren't all the same. An EMT is the less experienced first aid provider, and it's the first level of certi-fication. Someone who is certified as a paramedic, however, has completed another two-plus-years of intensive

A helmet's job is to sacrifice itself in order to protect you. When it takes a hard enough hit to crack the paint job as shown here, give it an honorable retirement and a place on your trophy shelf. It's done its job. Go buy a new one.

training and passed the accompanying certification tests.

Get Off the Track!

Reduce your chances of serious injury by doing a couple of simple things. The most important of these is to simply *get off the track!* If you crash or stall your bike on the racing line, get off the track immediately and get out of the way of following riders. Don't rely on the flaggers to protect you, because there's no guarantee they can or that they have even noticed you crashed. There are no statistics about the situation, but many riders get hurt not in the initial crash but from being hit while picking their bike back up, trying to get it restarted, and otherwise putting themselves and other riders in harm's way. GET OFF THE TRACK!

In the same vein, check into the first aid situation at the track. There should be a minimum of one staffed ambulance crew on hand from the beginning of practice through to the end of the day. If there's not, find out why by asking the promoter. An explanation of "we just call them when there's a problem" is not acceptable. Even a few minute's delay in treatment can be a life-or-death situation, and it could be your life we're talking about. All race promoters have an obligation to provide a staffed ambulance that is on hand at all times. Any promoters that do not are cutting corners and risking your life and health in order to save a few bucks. That's not someplace you want to be racing.

Nobody wants to become a statistic. Always think about the risk of injury when preparing to race or ride. Never ride alone or where no one knows you're there. There's no lonelier feeling than having a bad injury, being all by yourself, and being unable to call for help or even get back to your truck.

The Good Thing about Injuries

There's actually an upside to getting injured: It's a great motivator. Having to come back from an injury provides its own good reason to get serious about your training. Fate or plain old bad luck has handed you some time off from your normal routine and you can use it to focus on getting healthy, getting fit, and coming back to racing in better shape than ever before. Injuries force you to focus on your body and how to get it strong again. An injury is great motivation to train.

What follows is some advice about common dirt bike injuries, what you can expect, rehab times, and cautions. Since everyone is different and every injury is different, the advice here is intentionally very general.

Bone Fractures

A bone fracture (break) is one likely result of parting company with your bike at speed. An individual's vulnerability to fractures actually varies based on age. Men are actually less subject to fractures after age 45. However, kids break their bones easier, but they heal faster than adults.

A fracture is generally classified as either "simple," meaning that the skin is not broken, or "compound," when the skin is pierced and there's an open wound. Obviously, a compound fracture is much more severe and immediately painful, with the threat of both infection and blood loss accompanying the injury.

Some fractures heal faster than others. A fracture of the upper arm may heal in just a few weeks, while a fracture in the forearm can take much longer to knit together. Break your femur (thighbone), one of the longest and strongest bones in your body, and you can expect a long recovery because it takes a lot of force to cause a fractured femur. Broken wrists are especially common injuries because people instinctively—and incorrectly—use their arms to break a fall. Break is the operative word here.

Not that long ago, fractures were treated with heavy casts that were kept on for long periods of time to immobilize the entire limb. However, this treatment led to stiff joints and often permanent muscle weakness. Today, smaller functional braces that isolate the fracture while leaving joints free to move are considered a better choice. By allowing movement of the limb, stiffness is reduced or avoided completely and strengthening rehab exercises can begin immediately, leading to shortened recovery times.

Broken Ankle

Buy and wear the best motocross boots you can find. It's your first line of defense against lower leg and ankle injuries, which can knock you off the bike for several months. Lower leg injuries are slow to heal and a major nuisance.

A broken ankle is a break in one or both of the ankle bones (tibia and fibula). Unfortunately, racing provides plenty of interesting ways to fracture your ankle. Some of the symptoms include a snapping/popping noise when the injury occurs, intense pain (duh), swelling, bruising, and an ankle that doesn't like to have any weight put on it. You'll probably have no problem recognizing a broken ankle if it happens to you.

Because ankles are weight-bearing, immediate immobilization, elevation, and cold packs to reduce swelling are the first line of treatment even before you head off to the ER. Depending on the nature of the fracture, surgery may be necessary to get the bones back in proper alignment and a cast is pretty much a certainty in order to keep things immobilized long enough for the bones to have a chance to heal. You'll probably also have a chance to learn how to balance on crutches, and two to three months to get used to them.

Collarbones

If you had to pick one injury that every racer has endured, this would be the overwhelming choice. Let's see a show of hands here. What's that, you can't raise your hand? Collarbones are reportedly the most common broken bone in the human body because it only takes a mere 7 pounds of pressure to break it. You can generate that much pressure with your index finger. Collarbone breaks come in four flavors. Here's the best (so to speak) to the worst: (1) cracked, (2) splintered, (3) broken in two or more pieces, and (4) compound fracture (you don't want one of these).

Injuries are the price we pay to play with dirt bikes. The better shape you're in, the less chance you'll get hurt in the first place and the faster you'll recover and get back in the saddle.

Treatment is simple: See a doctor. This isn't one of those things that will heal itself if you can tough it out. You'll need the full course of X-rays, possible surgery, a sling, and rehab. A lot of racers try to come back from a broken collarbone too soon, only to re-injure the still-healing clavicle. Six weeks is the standard and minimum healing time you can expect. Let it heal. Kids typically heal quicker than veterans. Collarbone injuries are tricky because even when

you think they've healed, it pays to have an X-ray to confirm that the bones have knitted together. Otherwise, the first set of whoops you ride could re-break your collarbone.

Before you break your collarbone the next (or first) time, devote some of your strength training to such exercises as dumbbell shrugs, upright rows, and behind-the-neck presses. These exercises build strength and flexibility in the muscles around your collarbones.

115

ARM PUMP

Arm pump is technically not an injury, but a medical condition. When arm pump is bad, the pain and swelling can make your arms go rigid, possibly causing a crash. There appears to be many possible reasons for getting arm pump. Some people seem to be naturally prone to it, while others never experience it. As always, it seems that the better shape you're in, the less likely you are to have problems.

Some solutions:

• Ride a lot. Build up your forearms by putting in mucho seat time.

• Grip correctly. A death grip on the bars is a prelude to arm pump. Teach yourself to consciously loosen your grip as you ride. Use your legs more to control the bike and your arms less.

• Be well hydrated. When muscles are low on water, they tighten up and cramp. See The Nixon Test sidebar in Chapter 10 for details.

• Do the forearm and wrist exercises in Chapter 7, especially the wrist roller exercise.

• Carry one of the spring grip exercisers in your truck and use it during your daily commute.

• Set up your bike properly. Use a handlebar bend that makes the sitting-to-standing transition easy for your height. Experiment with bar bends (there's really only about a half-dozen different bends, no matter what names they stick on them) and bar heights. Experiment with different grips because some absorb vibration better. Aluminum oversize bars soak up vibes better than 7/8-inch bars. A steering stabilizer may also help. Get your suspension set up properly—read the manual and adjust accordingly or have it professionally prepped.

• Some riders swear by potassium as a cure. You can get plenty from orange juice, which also helps your hydration. Ditto with bananas and potatoes. Potassium is well regarded as a performance enhancing supplement, which is why bananas are a favored food of any jock.

• Finally, if you want to read a very well-researched and detailed article on the causes and possible solutions for arm pump, *Motocross Action* magazine did an excellent story on it in a 2001 issue. It's also available online in the archives file at www.motocrossactionmag.com. The surgical solution to arm pump is also discussed. This article is well worth a read if you suffer from arm pump on a regular basis.

Concussion

Concussions are brain injuries caused by a blow to the head; that trip over the handlebars will do it. There's a tendency to consider getting your "bell rung" as something to shrug off, but you shouldn't.

A concussion has some or all of these symptoms: confusion, disorientation, nausea, dizziness, bad headache, loss of balance, memory loss, and, of course, unconsciousness. These symptoms can appear either immediately or show up several days or even weeks after the injury. Any of these symptoms should be more than enough excuse to send you running to your doctor.

Since the physician can't put a bandage on your brain, the treatment is rest and maybe medication for the headache or nausea. "Rest" also means taking a break from racing. The minimum is at least a week for a mild concussion (you don't have to lose consciousness to get a concussion) to up to a month for a severe concussion. Repeated concussions are dangerous and may be a sign that you need to retire. Multiple concussions are suspected as one cause of Parkinson's disease and decreased mental function.

If you do get knocked out, it's also time to purchase a new helmet. Helmets protect your brain by sacrificing themselves. Once a helmet has absorbed a blow that's hard enough to leave you unconscious, its effectiveness is used up and it won't offer much protection the next time you hit the ground. So, while you're taking some time off from the moto-wars, go helmet shopping.

Gravel Rash

The primary risk with the everyday cuts and scrapes from racing is infection. Clean any wound thoroughly so that there's no remaining debris visible or by feel. Yes, this is going to hurt—it's supposed to. Once clean, apply an antiseptic such as Neosporin and bandage as necessary to keep it clean and protected. At least every other day, remove the bandage, apply more antiseptic, and re-bandage until the wound has closed.

If the wound doesn't close on its own or becomes red, puffy, oozes pus or just plain looks bad, it may be infected. Head for the nearest ER to have it checked. A severe infection from an otherwise minor wound can put you in the hospital . . . or the cemetery.

Ribs

Rib injuries are no fun because every breath you take is going to hurt. That gets old really fast.

Here's the thing about sore ribs: As long as you're not coughing up blood or having trouble breathing, there's not a whole lot that can be done beyond wrapping the ribs up tight and letting them heal at their own sweet pace. For a mild injury, you might end up in physical therapy instead, with no wrapping.

This isn't to say that you should take rib injuries lightly. Besides being painful, broken ribs can be more serious than they may seem at first. The real risk with broken ribs is that you've also damaged a lung (yes, you can bruise lungs) or you may have a rib poised to puncture a lung. You want to continue being able to breathe? Then see a doctor.

Quality knee braces like this Asterisk set aren't cheap ($500-plus) but it sure beats having your knee reconstructed by an orthopedic surgeon and spending six months on crutches. You'd spend that much for an exhaust pipe, so why aren't you spending it on injury prevention?

Prepare ahead of time for that day when you get to meet the emergency first aid crews first hand. Know where your health insurance card is located, a couple of phone numbers of people to contact, a riding buddy who can get your bike home, and any pre-existing medical problems or prescriptions that the medic should know about. Never ride at a track that doesn't have an ambulance and crew on hand.

Recovery time for rib injuries can be as quick as a couple of weeks, or can take two months or more. If you don't wear a chest protector, don't expect much sympathy from your racing buddies.

Shoulders

Shoulders are probably the best developed and strongest joint in the body. Compared to the knee joints, which are a work-in-progress, shoulders are a marvel of natural engineering.

The primary shoulder injury is to the rotator cuff, a group of tendons and muscles that hold your shoulder joint together and allow it to work so smoothly. Racers usually mess up their rotator cuffs by taking a hard fall landing with full force on their shoulder or arm. You can usually quickly confirm it's the rotator cuff that's been injured if there's immediate arm and shoulder

pain. Loss of movement, especially the ability to raise your hand above your head as if you're asking the teacher for permission, is also a clue.

Either partial or complete rotator cuff tears will require surgery if you want to regain full strength. Non-athletes will sometimes allow a rotator cuff

LEARN TO ROCK AND ROLL

Have you noticed how some racers seldom seem to get hurt in a crash, while others can barely touch the ground without ending up in a cast? The difference may be in knowing how to fall. Like most things in life, there's a right way and a wrong way to do it. Mother Nature gives us bad advice here, because most people instinctively stick their arms straight out when they fall. That's a sure-fire way to injure wrists, elbows, arms, and collarbones.

Practice falling. Learn to tuck and roll: Tuck your chin into your chest as you start to fall and keep your arms curled up rather than outstretched. Try to land on your shoulders and side; keep your arms and head tucked in until you stop moving. Sports that teach you how to fall correctly are gymnastics, skating, and martial arts. If you're injury-prone, you might want to give one of those sports a try as cross-training. Besides learning how to fall properly, you'll also become more flexible.

FOREARM WARM-UP

In the fight against arm pump, I'll offer up a martial arts stretching routine I've done for years on the start line to make sure my hands and forearms are loose and ready for action. Do it while you sit on the line waiting for the white flag to fly for the class ahead of you. Hold each stretch for a count of twenty and do both hands. You can do the whole routine in about a minute.

1. *Extend your arm and use one hand to bend down the fingers of the other arm as shown. Hold for a count of 20.*

2. *Using one hand to work the other, rotate the wrist back and forth with the palm facing down for a count of 20.*

3. *Finally, rotate the hand so the palm is facing out and hold it in a light stretch. Hold for a count of 20 and then switch hands and start with the other one.*

Lower leg injuries take a very long time to heal. Reduce the chances of getting one by investing in the best and most protective riding gear you can find. Get good boots like these, not the bargain specials.

hand. If you suspect you have a dislocated shoulder, put ice on it to reduce the swelling and pay a visit to the nearest emergency room. Treatment usually consists of a doctor repositioning the ball back into the joint, followed by immobilizing the arm in a sling or brace for two to three weeks. Physical therapy and rehab to strengthen shoulder muscles follows.

A *separated shoulder* is not the same as a dislocated shoulder. In a separation, the ligaments that hold your collarbone to the shoulder blade are torn. As with other shoulder injuries, a hard fall is all it takes. Clues that it's a separation are pain when the injury occurs, a misshapen shoulder, swelling or bruising, and limited shoulder movement with pain at the top of your shoulder where the collarbone (clavicle) meets the shoulder blade. Again, ice it down to reduce swelling and pain. Visit your doctor or the ER for X-rays to make sure it isn't a fracture. Separations are usually treated with slings and immobilization, although sometimes surgery is necessary. Healing is going to require six weeks and rehab.

Sprains

Sprains are injuries to a joint. You've stretched, torn, or otherwise tweaked a ligament, which is the tissue that holds adjoining bones together. It's possible to sprain any ligament, but the ankles, knees, and fingers are the most often

injury to partially heal without surgery, but going under the knife is the best plan for racers if you want your strength back. Rehab will begin immediately after surgery and continue for two to three months in order to restore strength, flexibility, and range of motion. Expect to be taking at least a three-month vacation from racing for a complete tear; or two months off for a partial tear.

A *dislocated shoulder* is what you have when the bones of your shoulder joint are moved apart so the joint no longer works. Basically, the ball-and-socket shoulder assembly has become two separate parts. A dislocated shoulder can be caused by a fall or any violent twisting of your upper arms. A dislocated shoulder makes itself known from the pain, weakness, a large bump, and numbness in the shoulder, arm, or

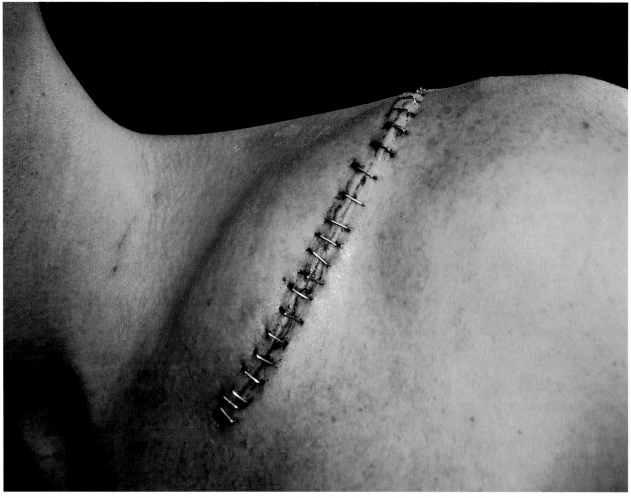

OUCH! Mess up your shoulder or collarbone and you may be looking at something like this. Cool scar though.

injured because these are the joints that get the most force applied to them. Catch your boot in a rut while you're on the gas, and you'll know exactly what this means.

Sprains are best treated with ice (20 minutes on, 20 minutes off) for the first 24 to 48 hours after the injury. Use the RICE approach: Rest, Ice, Compression, and Elevation. If the pain is severe or swelling is excessive, see your doctor. Without X-rays, it's hard to tell the difference between a sprain (which usually heals by itself) and a bone fracture. Your doctor will be able to tell for sure; however, you can probably skip the expense and hassle of an MRI. Ordinary sprains do not require a cast, crutches, surgery, or even continued medical care under a doctor's supervision once the problem has been successfully identified.

Sprains benefit from a light work out and stretching once swelling has subsided.

Wrists

It's easy to break a wrist because human nature mistakenly tells us to throw out our hands to cushion a fall. Helping to resist this urge is a good reason to take karate or jiu-jitsu. The thing is, Mom Nature never imagined we'd be sent flying from a bike traveling 35 miles per hour when she wrote the software that tells us to throw our arms out. That's the wrong way to fall—see the sidebar for the right way to do it—and our reward is a broken wrist.

Pain is immediate and swelling quickly follows. Your wrist will probably also show obvious deformation. An X-ray is necessary to determine the extent of the fracture. If it's not too severe, a simple

brace or cast may be all that's necessary, but it's not uncommon to expect surgery, rods, and screws to get everything reassembled and back in alignment.

Recovery time will vary depending on the severity of the injury, with two months being a typical minimum. Many riders try to come back from a broken wrist too quickly, relying on a cast or brace to support the injured area. Usually all this accomplishes is a delay of full healing and it sets the stage for possible re-injury.

Knee Injuries

Knee injuries are common in every active sport and they're especially prevalent in off-road riding with its combination of high speed, rough terrain, ruts, jumps, rocks, and plenty of

TOP TEN INJURY POTENTIAL*

You're most likely to get injured while riding when you're:

1. Showing off in the pits.
2. Passing someone faster than you who has slowed down for no apparent reason (there's always a reason).
3. Inviting friends, family or significant others along to watch the first race.
4. Wearing a new helmet for the very first time.
5. Riding alone on a long loop that's far, far away from your cooler.
6. Loading or unloading your bike (especially if you try to ride it up the ramp).
7. After a late-night, heavy-duty pre-ride bike maintenance session.
8. After saying to yourself and everyone else: "I'm only going to do one more lap."
9. Intentionally going slow and being extra-special careful because you're leaving on vacation the next day.
10. Telling your spouse you just bought a vintage Maico on eBay, you have to go pick it up, and it's 1,000 miles away.

*With thanks to "VintageDirt" on DirtRider.net

opportunities to accidentally kick yourself in the back of the head.

Knees are the body's weakest joint, especially if you're an athlete. They're the largest and most complex joint in your body and also the most poorly engineered. While shoulders have sturdy ball-and-socket designs that can take a lot of abuse, knees are a complex mess of bone, sinew, and cartilage that work almost in spite of itself. Knees are an evolutionary work-in-progress that would benefit from a full factory recall.

While we wait for the factory warranty program to kick in, realize that knees can benefit quite a bit from strength training to make them more stable and more resistant to injury. The flip side is that some types of training can cause a knee injury if done incorrectly. It's a balancing act and you need to know which side to be on.

Here's what to do to avoid or reduce knee problems:

• Exercise! Strengthening a knee begins with regular exercise, especially the quads (the big muscles on the top of your thighs) which help stabilize the knees.

• If you've had any kind of knee injury or surgery, you've got to do the rehab work diligently. Knees don't heal themselves. Resist the temptation to come back before your knee injury is fully healed because the chances of re-injury are high.

• Lighten up! Losing weight means your knees have to carry less of a load.

• Switch sides. If you always run on one side of the road or running track, reverse direction every other day. Otherwise you'll be prone to a repetitive-motion injury.

• Get knee braces. While a quality (i.e., expensive or doctor-prescribed) pair of knee braces may significantly reduce your chances of suffering a major knee injury, the jury is still out on whether this is true in all cases. Some people are biologically more susceptible to knee problems (my daughter is an example), while others never have a problem. Personally, any racer who doesn't wear substantial knee braces is kidding himself. At the very least, wear the best knee cups available, not the cheapo things that came with the pants. Knee injuries take a long time to heal, can be career-ending, and if surgery is required, you'll get to discover the (non-) joys of life on crutches.

Identifying and Treating Knee Injuries

• Bruises: Looks just like what it sounds like. Hurts like blazes and there's probably some swelling right away. Rest your leg and apply an ice pack for 15 minutes at a time.

• Runner's knee: There's a dull ache behind the knee cap that comes and goes, depending on the leg's position. Often simple strength exercises such as leg lifts, stretches for the quads and hamstrings, and some ice will be all you need to relieve the pain. If not, see your doctor.

• Knee sprains: Knees are linear things. They only like to move front to back, not side to side. Since a motocross track offers lots of possibilities to make a knee move in the wrong direction, that's why knee braces are recommended to limit the knee's movement within a safe range. A sideways blow to the knee can tear or stretch the ligament, creating a sprain, or cause the cartilage disks to tear. Pain will be immediate and swelling will follow. A minor sprain can be treated by immobilizing your leg and applying ice packs.

• The dreaded torn ACL: As the major stabilizing ligament in the knee, connecting the tibia to the femur, tearing the anterior cruciate ligament (ACL) is one injury you want to avoid. You'll need surgery to remove torn cartilage and repair the damage. Sometimes damage to the ligament will be so severe that it has to be rebuilt with a graft. Recovery from ACL surgery typically requires at least three months and your knee may never be as strong as it was before the injury.

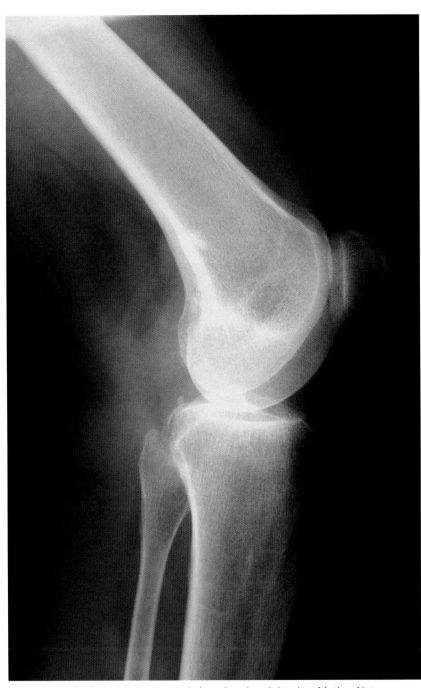

Knees are a complex, not-quite-ready-for-primetime joint that Mother Nature needs to re-engineer. That's why knees are so easily injured.

ICE TIME

When you're applying an ice bag to an injury, only use it for 15 minutes at a time. Apply it any longer, and your cells will kick into a survival mode that causes even more inflammation. Don't have an ice bag? Go to the grocery store and get some packages of frozen peas or corn. They're flexible and conform to whatever shape you need for the job.

TWO-MINUTE BOARD

- Don't tough out an injury. An injury that appears to be no big deal can hide a more severe internal injury.
- Wear good and protective riding gear. Like it or not, you're going to crash because everybody crashes.
- Being in good shape reduces the chances of getting hurt in the first place and you'll recover quicker from injuries.
- Purchase and wear knee braces. Knees are the body's weakest and easiest to injure joint. Braces may save you from three months on crutches.
- There are a lot of potential causes and solutions for arm pump. If you have this problem, work on developing your forearms, stretch before each moto, and stay hydrated. Also be sure your bike is properly set up.

SAMPLE WORK OUT PLAN

Use a work out planner like this one to track your progress as you go—it's easy to over- or underestimate how much you are training if you don't write it down.

Workout Plan Week of 10/24 to 10/30

CORE WORKOUT	√	Monday	Tuesday	Wednesday	Thursday	Friday	Saturday	Sunday
crunches	✓	200		200		200		
raised leg pushup	✓	20		20		20		
Superman	✓	10		10		10		
chin-up	✓	10		10		10		
wall sit	✓	1 minute		1 minute		1 minute		
calf raises	✓	35		35		35		

STRENGTH WORKOUT	√	Monday	Tuesday	Wednesday	Thursday	Friday	Saturday	Sunday
lat pull-down	✓		150# 2 sets		150# 2 sets			
hammer curl	✓		35# 2 sets		35# 2 sets			
leg press	✓	255# 3 sets →			255# 3 sets			
hamstrings	✓	125# 3 →			125# 3 sets			
lat pull-up	✓		140# 2		140# 2			
shoulder press	✓							
bench press	✓		165# 3X		165# 3X			
row	✓		185# 4X		205# 3X			
woodchopper	✓		110# 2X					
Quads	✓		145# 3X		145# 3X			

ENDURANCE WORKOUT	√	Monday	Tuesday	Wednesday	Thursday	Friday	Saturday	Sunday
hill route	✓	7 miles		7 miles hill route		Run Like Hell 5K	HASH 5 miles	
intervals	—			NEXT WEEK—				REST DAY
DAY'S DISTANCE:		7		7		3.1	5	
WEEK'S TOTAL:							22.1	
TOTAL TO DATE:							1,150	
			※ order new shoes!					

GLOSSARY

- Andipose tissue: Another word for fat.
- Aerobic: In the presence of oxygen.
- Aerobic exercise: Anything that involves movement and rapid breathing (no, not that . . .). This is a repetitive exercise that causes your body to call for more oxygen and your heart and lungs work harder to meet the demand.
- Anaerobic training: The opposite of aerobic, requiring short bursts of power from your muscles rather than endurance. Strength training, if you prefer short words.
- Arthritis: Inflammation of the joints. Often results from broken bones over time. Very un-fun.
- Atrophy: What happens to your muscles when you do nothing more active than channel surf.
- BMI: Body Mass Index. A way of mathematically determining whether you're fit or fat, according to government standards. And we all know how reliable government standards are, right? Actually not a bad measurement, but you need to understand how it works.
- Bench number: The amount of weight you claim (loudly) you can bench press. Also the subject of more outright lies and sheer exaggeration than two political conventions put together. It's also totally meaningless in the real world of racing.
- Body-fat measurement: There are several ways to measure this and all of them provide slightly different numbers. If you use a body-fat measurement to gauge your progress, be sure to use the same method all the time.
- Bursitis: Inflammation of the bursa, a fluid-filled sac in your joints that lubricates things and keeps you mobile. Hurts like heck, so go easy on exercises and sports that over-stress your joints.

- Calorie: The single most misunderstood measurement of energy in recorded history. It's a unit of energy and different foods contain different amounts of this energy. All you need to remember is that a gram of fat is 9 calories; a gram of carbohydrate or protein is 4 calories; and the average-sized male rarely needs more than 2,000 calories a day. You can do the math from there.
- Clavicle: The collarbone, easily the most frequently broken bone in dirt biking.
- Concussion: A hard blow to your brain that knocks you unconscious and essentially bruises your brain. Anytime you get one, that's a cue to buy a new helmet and take some time off. A lot of concussions probably means you need to think about retiring from racing because your long-term health is at risk.
- Empty calories: The kind you get from food and drink that have no nutritional value. Sure they taste good, but they're not good for you. Empty calories may not have any nutritional value, but they still will be converted into fat. Lots of it.
- Fartlek: A Swedish term meaning to alternate between your normal running pace and a faster pace. Very useful in training drills.
- Glucose: Blood sugar, which is what burns fat to produce energy for your muscles. That's good, but you don't want to have too much because then it just gets stored away and converted into fat.
- Heat stroke: Your body's temperature-adjusting mechanisms have shut down, you no longer sweat, you're confused, your core temperature is way up, and you're way close to dying.

- Heat exhaustion: You're still a few steps shy of heat stroke. Basically you're dehydrated and too hot. Stop doing whatever you're doing and find some shade and water, pronto. By the way, you're going to wake up tomorrow really, really tired and sore as hell.
- Isometric exercise: Exercises performed against an immovable object like a wall. Your muscles contract but the joints don't move.
- Lactic acid (lactate): The byproduct of aerobic exercise and the reason your muscles get tired. Endurance training makes your muscles able to tolerate higher levels of lactic acid.
- Lactate threshold (LT): When your muscles can no longer do much because they're overwhelmed with lactic acid. Training moves this point further away.
- Maximum heart rate (HRMax): This is as fast as your heart can go, and your personal redline after which the valves float.
- Maximum oxygen consumption (VO2 max): Your maximum aerobic capacity, since it reflects the maximum amount of oxygen your body can process during exercise. Training increases (or should if you're doing it right) your VO2 max.
- Muffin: Another word for cake. Doesn't matter what it's made from, it's still cake.
- Muscle endurance: The muscle's ability to do something repeatedly. For racing you need both muscular endurance and strength. One without the other won't do the job.
- Muscle strength: The maximum force you can put out in one single effort. Unless all you're doing is lifting weights, strength alone isn't enough. You need endurance too.

- 1RM or 1RMax: The maximum weight you can lift one time, with proper form.
- Rep: Short for repetition; one complete movement of an exercise.
- RICE: Rest, Ice, Compression (bandages), Elevation. This is how you treat most musculoskeletal injuries like sprains.
- Set: Weight-lifting lingo for a fixed number of reps.
- Side stitch: A sharp pain in the side when you're not getting enough air to your respiratory system. Not fatal and easily cured on the run by making weird grunting noises.
- Sprain: Twisting a joint in a direction Mother Nature didn't intend. We've all been there. Can hurt like hell and swelling can be severe, but it won't kill you. Treat it with RICE.
- Speed work: Running laps on a running track at close to your maximum speed. Besides making you stronger, it teaches your muscles how to deal with lactic acid buildup.
- Warm-up: A prelude to more vigorous exercise. If it doesn't put some sweat on your forehead, then it's not a warm-up and you're just wasting your time.

INDEX

**Yamaha YZF & WRF
Performance Projects**
ISBN 0-7603-2140-X

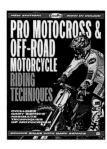

**Pro Motocross and Off-Road
Riding Techniques**
ISBN 0-7603-1802-6

**Motocross and Off-Road
Performance Handbook**
ISBN 0-7603-1975-8

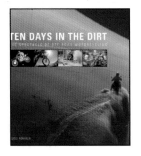

Ten Days in the Dirt
ISBN 0-7603-1803-4

Motocross America
ISBN 0-7603-2179-5

**Motocross Racers:
30 Year of Legendary Dirt Bikes**
ISBN 0-7603-1239-7

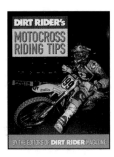

**Dirt Rider's Motocross
Riding Tips**
ISBN 0-7603-1315-6

**Freestyle Motocross:
Jump Tricks from the Pros**
ISBN 0-7603-0926-4

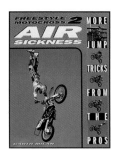

**Freestyle Motocross 2:
Air Sickness**
ISBN 0-7603-1184-6